ROMAN BRICK AND TILE

Frontispiece

Reconstruction of the Bath House, Beauport Park

ROMAN BRICK AND TILE

GERALD BRODRIBB, PH.D, F.S.A.

Alan Sutton Publishing
Brunswick Road, Gloucester

First Published 1987

© Gerald Brodribb 1987

British Library Cataloguing in Publication Data

Brodribb, Gerald
  Roman brick and tile : an analytical survey
  and corpus of surviving examples.
  1. Bricks, Roman—England—Catalogs
  2. Tiles, Roman—England—Catalogs
  3. England—Antiquities—Roman—Catalogs
  I. Title
  691'.4   DA145

ISBN 0-86299-363-6

Typesetting and origination by
Alan Sutton Publishing Limited
Printed in Great Britain

To
Mark Singleton,
the owner of Beauport Park
without whose co-operation this book
would not have been possible.

The author acknowledges with thanks that the publication of this book has been assisted by grants from the Marc Fitch Fund and the Twenty-Seven Foundation.

LIST OF CONTENTS

LIST OF ILLUSTRATIONS

ACKNOWLEDGEMENTS

I wish to thank all those Curators of Museums and Directors of Archaeological Units who have so readily given me access to the Roman Brick and Tile in their charge and made me so welcome to study it. My thanks go also to the following who have in many ways given me assistance and encouragement :

Ian Betts	William Manning
Ernest Black	Alan McWhirr
George Boon	David Peacock
Conant Brodribb	Tony Rook
Michael Brodribb	Peter Seymour
Bernard Charles	Mike Stone
Barry Cunliffe	Graham Webster
Henry Cleere	David Whitehouse
Roy Friendship-Taylor	Roger Wilson
Christopher Green	Alan Wood
Mark Hassall	

and also thanks to my wife Jessica for her constant interest and help in research and for proof-reading.

ILLUSTRATIONS

I am most grateful to Guy de La Bédoyère for his work on the drawings and to the following for permission to use the following illustrations:

No. 3 (American Journal of Archaeology), 16 (Society of Antiquaries of London), 21 (Roy Friendship-Taylor), 28 and 38 (The Canterbury Archaeological Trust), 30 and 40 (Dr R.J.A. Wilson), 50 (The Museum of London), 51 and 52 (The Surrey Archaeological Society), 54 (Conant Brodribb), 55 (4 and 5 Dr D. Baatz, 7 Dr O. Hoffman) 56 (The National Museum of Wales), 60 (The Trustees of the British Museum) : also a quotation from Gerald of Wales on p. 50 (Penguin Books).

INTRODUCTION

At an early date in the excavations at Beauport Park in East Sussex tile carrying the stamp of the *Classis Britannica* was found, and it was decided that every scrap of tile should be very carefully looked at. At present over thirteen tons of tile and brick have been analysed in various types – all from a bath-house building that covered an area of only 114 square metres. In the apparent absence of any serious robbing this seemed a unique opportunity to study tile in detail and to assess an undisturbed collection. This work gradually expanded to cover details of nearly 6000 items of complete or unusual tile gathered from over 460 sites in Britain (see appendix i). The list I have made represents, however, only a fraction of the original quantity used. Time and destruction have waged a heavy toll : for instance, it was estimated that some 43,000 *tegulae* were used on the roof of the Palace at Fishbourne, but less than half-a-dozen survive complete. It is also revealing to consider that all the 620 complete *tegulae* recorded on the list would not be enough to roof one small bath-house. Recently, however, there has been a new awareness of what can be discovered from a careful study of tile : features such as varieties of flange and cut-out on *tegulae*, signature marks found on the face, tally-marks cut on the edge, individual types of combing on box and other tile, and rare varieities such as 'half-boxes' and 'arm-chair' voussoirs. The Tile and Brick conference organised by Alan McWhirr at Leicester in April 1979 did much to arouse interest, and as a result current reports are now showing some mention of tile.

   I hope this pioneer survey will enable others to spot the various features, and persuade excavators to look hard at tile before discarding it. Tile terminology has never been properly considered, and the policy here has been to make a clear distinction between types, and to use wherever possible the original classical name e.g. *bessalis* and *lydion*.

   Though a number of classical writers have been quoted, they do not provide much detailed information about tile and brick. There is only one surviving work devoted to the matter of building, the *De Architectura*, a treatise in ten books that L. Vitruvius Pollio wrote in his old age with a dedication to Augustus and dated to about 14 B.C. He may have been a military engineer under Julius Caesar during the African War of 46 B.C. Because of its early date *De Architectura* can only deal with buildings of pre-Imperial times, but for all its limitations it is a valuable source book. It includes for example a section on the preparation of clay in the making of bricks, though this mainly concerned sun-dried bricks – *lateres crudi* – and there is only a passing allusion to kiln-baked bricks, which were not widely used until after the time of Vitruvius. During the Republic, private houses and public buildings were generally built of bricks that had not been baked in a kiln, and these sun-dried bricks not only tended to collapse when subjected to moisture, but were thick and clumsy and took up much space. There are in Britain only a few surviving examples of partially-fired mid-first century and pre-conquest bricks. At Leicester the Jewry Wall museum has a *lydion* which came from a wall of clay brick set in sand above a masonry footing. At Colchester a similar construction was found in a building destroyed in the Boudiccan revolt of A.D. 61, and there were also a few examples of native bricks, including two very thin tiles, one of which bore a moulded boss (Hawkes and Hull, 1947, 347). From the Belgic site at Prae Wood near Verulamium there are fragments of early, possibly pre-Roman, bricks inadequately fired and smoothed over by hand leaving finger impressions. The general appearance and texture could be compared with overbaked shortbread (Wheeler and Wheeler, 1936, 178 and pl.lvi).

A good example of mid-first century brick comes from Quinton : it measures 330 mm × 350 mm × 37 mm and is roughly made of brown untempered clay. The Roman site at Baldock has also produced fragments of brick, some of which are pre-Claudian in date. By the end of the first-century A.D. the Romans brought the art of making baked brick to perfection and introduced it wherever they went, adapting style and method according to circumstances.

It is evident that the size of the various types of tile and brick were based upon the unit of the Roman foot. An *uncia* means a one-twelfth part of anything, and 12 *unciae* (inches) amounted to one Roman foot (*pes*). According to Hultsch (1882, 1971 ed. 700) the Roman *pes monetalis* was the equivalent of 295.7 mm (or 11.64 English inches). The Romans were unable to measure very accurately, and in the Museum of London some foot rules can be seen marked in quarters (*palmae*) twelfths (*unciae*) and sixteenths (*digiti*). It is doubtful if Roman tile-makers in Britain bothered with such instruments, and indeed any attempt to produce matching tiles to an

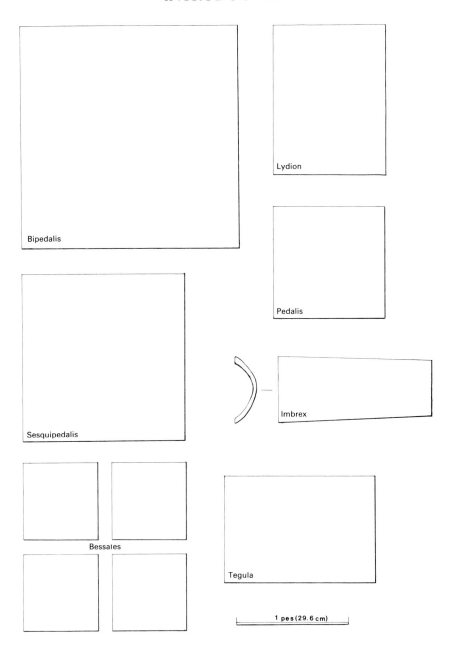

1 Comparative sizes of Brick and Tile

exact standard was greatly complicated by the problem of shrinkage as a result of the firing of the tile in the kiln. Personal experiment has shown that a block of clay will steadily shrink as it dries out, and the process of baking will intensify this up to a degree of some 10% loss of the original size. Even the position of the tile in the kiln could produce variations of shrinkage. Apart from this problem, we must remember that every tile is an individual man-made object : so long as the tile could fulfil its purpose, a small discrepancy of size would not matter.

In spite of the huge loss of brick and tile over the post-Roman years, it is surely not too late to attempt to extract valuable evidence from what is after all the commonest of all Roman remains. Fresh material is still coming to light, and at long last it is being looked at instead of being instantly cast on the spoil heap. An excellent method of processing tile has been suggested (Young, 1979).

I regard this present work as a mere starting point for further recording and research by others, and I would welcome any information from readers concerning the subject.

Gerald Brodribb
  Stubbles
    Ewhurst Green
      East Sussex.

CHAPTER 1

ROOFING-TILES

TEGULA

(a) History

Pliny informs us that tiles (*tegula* – a small covering) were invented by a Greek called Cinyra, son of Agrippa, on the island of Cyprus, but he gives no dates. (Pliny, VII, 56, 195). In Greece tiled roofing goes back to at least the second millennium B.C., and a rare example of Helladic tile can be seen in the Langley Tile Museum in London. It measures 230 × 190 mm and is without flanges (cf. Vitruvius' reference to 'tegulae sine marginibus', V, 10, 3). The tile comes from the House of Tiles at Lerna, near Argos, in Greece, and it is said :

> These Lerna tiles are probably the earliest baked clay roof tiles that have been identified anywhere in the world. They must date from about 1800 B.C., or earlier . . . The supposition is that the tiles were laid overlapping on a bed of clay which served as mortar, with a relatively slight slope.
>
> (Dobson, 1960, 12 & pl. 20)

By the 6th century BC flat tiles (*tegulae*), now with flanges, were used in conjunction with cover-tiles (*imbrices*) not only in Greece, but in Italy as well. These early flanged *tegulae* varied considerably in size, the largest being 1150 mm long × 850 mm wide and the smallest 360 mm × 315 mm; the average size was about 410 mm × 360 mm (Blake, 1947, 304).

There are many examples of roof tiles from the Greek cities of southern Italy and Sicily. Some of the earliest ones, found at San Mauro, come from a temple and are decorated and painted, but even finer are the *tegulae* to be seen at Paestum. They form the roof of a tomb, the Hypogean Sacellum, which was originally covered over and buried, and has not been exposed. The tomb probably dates to

2   The Hypogean Sacellum at Paestum, Italy

509 BC when the Sybarites took refuge in Paestum. The Sacellum is
a shallow structure that rises only about four feet from the present
ground level, and is covered by twenty *tegulae* in two rows of five on
each side. Nineteen of these *tegulae* are original, the twentieth being
an obviously new replacement fitted with a hinge to afford entrance
to the tomb. The *tegulae* are very large, measuring 1100 mm × 760
mm with flanges 45 mm wide and an external depth of 80 mm. The
cut-outs at the bottom are square and 90 mm long. Since the building
was meant to be covered and was never open to the weather, there
are no *imbrices* to cover the flanges. These *tegulae* are probably the
oldest to survive *in situ*. The Greek examples predate any Roman
tiling by several hundred years.

The roofs (*tecta*) at Rome were originally covered with straw, and
examples of these were preserved down to the Imperial period in the
'Casa Romuli' and another hut placed in the citadel. To quote
Vitruvius, these 'were shrines covered with straw which can remind
us, and signify the customs and antiquities of Rome' (Vit. II 1, 5).
Virgil also refers to 'the house of Romulus, freshly thatched with
straw' (Aeneid, VIII, 654). Straw was later superseded by wooden

shingles (*scandulae*), because they rose so named like steps one above the other. *Scandulae* are referred to by Columella (De Rei Rustica, VIII 3, 6), by Vitruvius (II, 1, 4) and by Pliny (XVI, 15, 36), where he says that 'hard oak was the most suitable for roof shingles'. Several shingles made of oak have recently been found near the bath-house at Beauport Park in England.

Roofs made of wood were a considerable fire risk, and Livy states that, because of this, tiles (*tegulae*) were eventually supplied at the state's expense (History, v. 55.3). The *tegula* was a very heavy object, and could become dangerous: Plutarch tells the story of how King Pyrrhus lost his life in 272 BC during an attack on Argos in Greece, 'When a woman saw her son engaged in conflict with Pyrrhus, she lifted a tile with both hands, and threw it at him. The tile fell on his head below the helmet and crushed his vertebrae'. (Parallel Lives, xxxiv, 2). Another unfortunate victim was little Pastor, the grandson of the poet Ausonius. He died when a workman repairing a roof threw down a tile which hit the boy and killed him. Ausonius wrote a memorial poem about Pastor (Parentalia XI). There are a number of less violent references to *tegulae* by the classical writers, especially the playwright Plautus (ob.184 BC).

There are few references to *tegulae* in inscriptions, but one (Dessau 3400) refers to a gift of 'tegulas aeneas auratas', and another tells of a gift to a temple of 'tegulas CCCC tectas', possibly also made of bronze. Other references suggest that the cost of providing *tegulae* for a building was borne by some benefactor, while a tombstone inscription relates how a man met his death when 'tegula Romae prolapsa peremit', '*he died at Rome from a falling tile*' (CIL, iii, 2083).

It is very rare to find the word *tegula* incorporated in a tile stamp, but two stamps on tile found at Chester in 1972 state that 'Aulus Viducius (?) made this roof-tile (*tegulam*) for Legio XX in the third consulship of Verus' i.e. in A.D. 167 (Brit. 9. 1978, 476, item 16). Variants based on the word *tegula* include the adjective *tegulicius* meaning 'covered with tile' as found in the inscription 'Deo Mercurio attegiam teguliciam compositam Severinus Satullinus C.T. ex voto posuit L L M', *Severinus Satullinus, tribesman of the Triboci built (this) shrine made of brick for the god Mercury in accordance with his vow, joyfully, willingly and deservedly.*' (Dessau 3204). Another word, *tegularius*, found in the inscription beginning 'P. Anicius P.L. Eros Tegularius' (CIL X, 3729), would seem to mean 'Tile-maker'.

The roof *tegula* was such a common and essential object that it could be reckoned almost as a yard-stick of possessions and wealth. According to the Charter of Tarentum (89 BC) no one could be a

3   An in-situ roof at Herculaneum, Italy

member of the municipal Senate or vote in the Senate unless he
possessed within the confines of Tarentum a dwelling roofed with at
least 1500 tiles, clearly a measure of substance. In a similar way, the
Charter of Urso (44 BC) required local councillors to possess a house
of sufficient value to provide a pledge. Such value was based upon
the quantity of roofing tiles. As further evidence of *tegula* valuation
the Senators in Rome in 43 BC contributed to the war fund by an
assessment of four asses per roof tile (Dio Cassius, Hist. XLVI, 31, 3).
This consideration recalls the way in which in much later times in
England a tax was imposed on the quantity of windows a house
possessed.

    There are now few examples where it is possible to study the roofs
of ancient buildings whose tiles are still intact and in their original
position, but in the peristyle of the Villa dei Misteri in Pompeii a

small structure has survived roofed by four *tegulae* measuring 560 ×
490 mm : these were taken down carefully so that the ash could be
removed, and they were then put back in place (Maiuri, 1931,
68–83). Herculaneum has also provided at least one example of the
original roofing still *in situ*, and the reason for this rare survival was
that

> The city was swamped by torrents of volcanic mud in a semi-fluid state,
> which thus penetrated into the houses, and filled them up to the ceilings,
> without causing the roofs to collapse. As a consequence of this action a
> tile roof of one of the houses was still intact and in place at the moment of
> excavation, being supported by a solid mass of hardened volcanic mud
> beneath.

This roof was over the house of Telaio (Insula V, iv, 3–4) (Van
Buren, 1941, 469 & fig 16). Two other intact roofs have recently
been found : one at the Villa Regina at Boscoreale, and the other in
the peristyle of the House of Julius Polybius at Pompeii.

Tile roofing could not become really efficient until the *tegula* had
developed a flange with cut-outs at top and bottom, which enabled
both a snug fit, and a taper which helped to lock the tiles together.
The nature of such a structure meant that the roof would have to be
built up from the bottom course towards the apex. Not having any

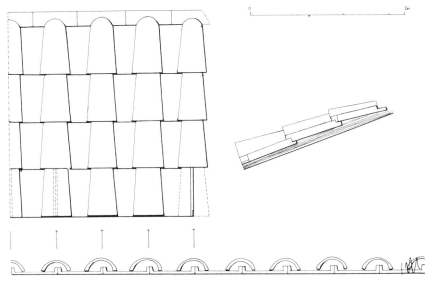

4   The construction of a roof with *tegulae* and *imbrices*

hook or nib to attach to the rafters the tiles would have to sit in position by sheer weight and friction. Once the *imbrices* were fitted over the gaps, and with cement between the flanges, the roof would become virtually one solid piece. The pitch would have to be sufficient to allow rainwater to flow off, yet not steep enough to create any tendency to slip.

The roof over the Sacellum at Paestum was set at 25 degrees, and though this was not built as an external roof it might well give evidence of normal practice. Vitruvius in describing a temple of Tuscan order states that the pitch of the roof was 'one in three' (*tertario*), or 30 degrees (IV, 7, 5). Any increase of degree of pitch on a roof would naturally mean an increase in the number of tiles required. This works out at : 10 degree pitch (1.5 per cent increase), 20 degree pitch (6 per cent increase), 30 degree pitch (15 per cent increase), and 40 degree pitch (30 per cent increase).

It has been observed by A.G. Rook (1979, 295) that present day *tegula* and *imbrex* roofs in Italy have a slope of about 20 degrees except when they cover a vault, as in churches. His experiments with tiles set on planed wooden boards showed that the angle of repose was about 40 degrees and my own experiments have shown that *tegulae* do not tend to slip until an angle of at least 30 degrees is passed.

(b)   Features

Every *tegula* has certain characteristics which tend to vary with individual examples: these can sometimes identify the handiwork of a particular tile-maker, quite apart from any 'signature' that may be present. Different sites can produce *tegulae* with similar characteristics, and this helps to identify the source, and could provide useful dating evidence.

1.   Nail holes

These holes, round or square in equal proportion, can be as large as 13 mm, but the average is about 7 mm. They are usually centrally placed, and not more than 50 mm from the top edge, though on a Binchester example the hole is set to one side. The holes were generally pierced before firing, and there are at least four examples of a nail remaining, corroded but intact: from Piddington, Brading, and Silchester, while another *tegula* from Lydney has a nail intact in its hole almost touching the flange, which suggests that there was once another on the other side as well. In the Piddington example the hole has been chopped out after the tile was fired, knocking off a large round portion of tile on the underside, but this is rare.

There are certain oddities. A large *tegula* from Dover has two nail holes on the same level near the top, an example from Colchester has the hole nearer the bottom than the top, while examples from Winchester and Holt have holes in the centre. One tile from Crookhorn has as many as six holes scattered over the face, another unprovenanced *tegula* in the Ashmolean Museum has four holes below the line of centre, while one from Fishbourne has a single hole 50 mm from the bottom edge.

Of the 615 complete *tegulae* recorded one in five carried holes : the obvious conclusion is that only certain *tegulae* were attached, and those most likely would be the tiles of the lowest course overhanging the eaves. Since holes were made before firing some policy must have been adopted in the manufacture to ensure that the tiler received the correct proportion of nailable tiles. Evidence for the attachment of the lowest course comes from the contract known as Lex Puteolana (105 BC) (CIL I, 698) which says that 'tegulas primores omnes in antepagmento ferro figito marginem imponito'.

Two fragments of *tegulae* (from Weeting and Lympne) are most unusual in that each carries a hole which was afterwards blocked by a circular pad of clay 30 mm in diameter: this does not plug the hole but merely seals the end of it. A blocking pad such as this is quite different from the raised rim found on tiles from Brading and Titsey where the clay pushed down to make the hole has been flattened out to form an evenly shaped rim below the hole.

2. *Weight and size*

The total weight of any roofing must have been very considerable. Experiments have been made with *tegulae* from the Beauport Park collection. The average weight of 41 complete *tegulae* found there works out at 13.6 lbs (29.98 kg) each, and the average weight of a similar number of *imbrices* works out at 5.6 lbs (12.34 kg). A hypothetical section of roof covering 15m² would require 160 *tegulae* set in four rows of 40 each, and this assumes there were no gaps for cement. The weight of this section of roof would therefore be 160 × 13.6 lbs, which equals 2176 lbs (4797 kg). The number of *imbrices* would be eight less because of the two ends where *imbrices* are not needed so the weight of them would be 152 × 5.6 lbs, which comes to 672 lbs (1481 kg). Together these roofing tiles would weight over a ton (1.016 tonnes), and to this would have to be added the weight of the tiles along the ridge, cement around the *imbrices* (i.e. torching), nails (if any), and antefixes (if any).

Assessment of roof weight has also been made with *tegulae* from Caerleon measuring 550 mm × 380 mm and weighing 25 lbs (55 kg) each with *imbrices* 550 mm long and weighing 8 lbs (17.6 kg) each. This shows that the total weight of tiles on a roof covered by smaller *tegulae* is not much different from that of a roof covered by larger tiles. (Gentry, 1976, 37)

With this knowledge of size and weight, it becomes possible to estimate the total number of roof tiles required for any building. At Beauport Park for example it is estimated that about 1100 *tegulae* were needed for the roof (114 m^2); by using various methods it is possible to say with confidence that some 650 *tegulae* have already been accounted for. This is a very high percentage. As has already been mentioned, a note in the museum at Fishbourne states that 43000 *tegulae* may have been needed to cover the roof of the whole vast building: three only have survived quite complete, which demonstrates the degree of destruction and robbing that many Roman buildings have suffered.

Mention has been made of some unusually large *tegulae*. There are less than ten sites which have produced *tegulae* with a length of over 500 mm. The two longest are one from Caerleon which measures 570 mm long × 380 mm wide, and an even bigger one from Silchester which measures 570 mm long × 480 mm wide, producing an area of 0.27 m^2 which must surely make it the largest *tegula* found in Britain, though even this cannot match some *tegulae* found elsewhere in the Empire. At the other end of the range there is a *tegula* from Piddington which is only 310 mm long × 270 mm wide, and several *tegulae* from Dorchester (Dorset), Caistor by Norwich, and Silchester which are only 330 mm long.

An early scientific attempt to measure the density of tile was made by a Mr. J. Webster F.S.A. in 1768. He tested for porosity on four examples of tile: a Roman tile heavily baked and one more lightly baked, brick of *c*.1620, and a 'modern' tile of 1767. His test showed that the Roman tile was more dense than the others, and therefore less porous. (1775, 184–7)

3   The flange

The tile-maker had several other functions to perform apart from making the occasional hole in the face of the *tegula*. First the flanges would have to be created. Personal experiment has shown that these can be created by folding up the edges of the clay in the mould or former, and then slicing away the surplus clay. It is often possible in a broken section to see how the clay is curved-up to create the flange.

As a rule, the average depth of the flange works out at double the depth of the face of the *tegula*, i.e. the cross-section of the unflanged part of the body. The average depth of the external flange is 50 mm – almost exactly one-sixth of the Roman foot. It is rare to find a *tegula* with a face that has a thickness of under 20 mm, but one from Ickham is only 14 mm thick, while one from Slonk Hill is 18 mm thick. It must be remembered that many *tegulae* have considerable variations of thickness at different points of the face. The figures here concern the centre point of the lower edge.

On a few occasions the internal depth of the flange is less than the depth of the face, e.g. a Garden Hill example has a flange only 10 mm deep, mounted on a face that is 35 mm deep. Other examples of a deep face carrying a flange that is much shallower include those from Fishbourne and Chichester which both have faces as deep as 38 mm, and the Chichester example has a flange of only 22 mm mounted on it. In contrast to this there are some flanges that are considerably deeper than the face. An example from Heddington has a flange 40 mm deep on a face that is only 9 mm thick; a *tegula* from Chelmsford has a 45 mm flange mounted on a 15 mm face.

Some flanges are stepped or sloped at the top end, while in other cases the flange at the top end has been chamfered off before firing for a length of some 55 mm. The purpose of this chamfering seems obscure since it would simply cause the *tegula* above to slide down.

In several examples the outside edge of the underside of the flange has been chamfered off for the whole length of the *tegula*, and is not just part of the cut-away at the lower end. This bevelled edge has no obvious purpose. There are also examples where the top of the flange at the lower end has been chamfered off at 45 degrees for a distance of about 20 mm.

The flange itself is subject to considerable variation of shape and thickness. It is usually rounded at the top on the inside. Some flanges are quite flat and squared off. Some are much wider at the bottom than at the top. An example from Chester tapers from 40 mm at the bottom to only 17.5 mm at the top. There can also be great contrasts in width.

In an example from Chelmsford, the top of the flange measures only 7.5 mm across, and one from Richborough is almost as narrow

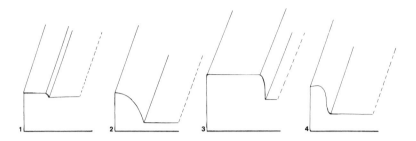

5   Contrasts in depth and width of the flanges (Scale ⅓)
   1. Garden Hill;   2. Heddington;   3. Fishbourne;   4. Chelmsford

at 8 mm. Sometimes these very thin flanges tend to bend inward at top end as seen in examples from Burham and Neatham.

It is common for the whole *tegula* to be wider at the top than at the bottom, and when this variation becomes extreme, as in an example from Chichester where the difference is 60 mm, the angle of the flanges takes on almost a V-shaped appearance.

Apart from variations in thickness some flanges have notable differences in profile and at times the maker has allowed fancy to prevail as some rather exotic examples show. If these examples seem strange it may be of interest to consider for comparison some given by Chauffin in his survey of tile from the Bas-Dauphiné region of France. He suggests that flanges of *tegulae* of the earliest time (the Bonne-Epoque of the first to third century) are more square-cut and have far less variety than those of later times. (1956, 81–8, & pl.11)

4   *Flanges deliberately removed*

There are a number of examples where the flanges on the *tegulae* have been deliberately removed by chipping. The purposes of this would seem to be to make the *tegulae* more readily usable as flat tiles for flooring or bonding purposes. When used to make up a floor the *tegula* thus treated is usually laid face downwards, so as not to show the chipped edges; at Paestum however the floor of one of the rooms in the Baths is covered with the deflanged *tegulae* laid face upwards thus revealing the marks where the flanges were chipped away. At Pompeii there are examples of flanges having been neatly sawn off instead of being hacked away.

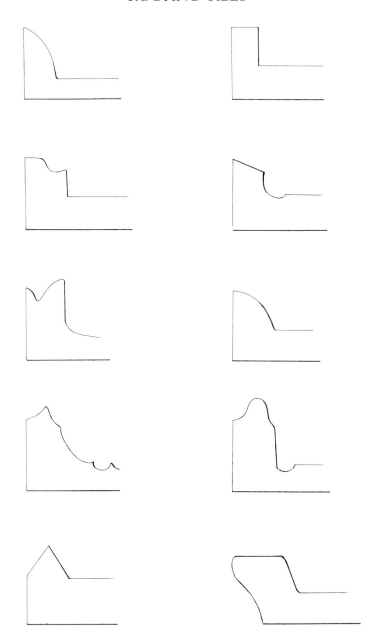

6 Variations of flange profiles from British sites. (Scale ¼)

5   *Grooves inside flange*

There is usually a single finger-made groove in the angle between the inside of the flange and the face of the *tegula*. This may be part of the natural way of finishing off the making of the flange, or it may be intended to assist the out-flow of rain water. A double groove instead of a single one occurs on only 14 out of the complete *tegulae* examples listed (2.5 per cent): on 23 examples there is no groove at all (4.2 per cent), the others all have the single groove. An example from Weeting has a single groove, but the edge has a double lip to it which seems to have been made with something other than a finger. A unique fragment from Letchworth has as many as three grooves.

6   *Cut-aways*

It is necessary for all *tegulae* to have cut-away sections at both bottom and top of the flange to enable the tiles to slot into each other and thus form a solid and secure block. The top end of the *tegula* is often wider than the bottom (the average difference is 27 mm), and this helps the *tegulae* to fit more easily together.

The cut-away of the flange at the top averages 50 mm in length,

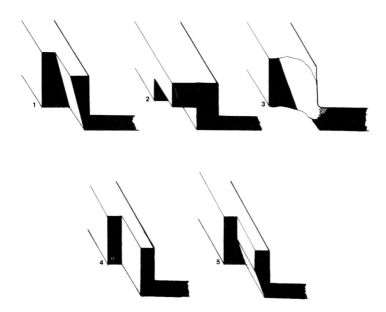

7   Various forms of cut-awasys at bottom end of flange. (Scale *c.* ⅙)

and normally consists of the complete removal of the end of the flange to make it level with the face. On some *tegulae* it seems that the cutting of both ends has been done simultaneously with a long knife in a way which leaves the appearance of a scraped area right across the *tegula*. There are examples of such a marking on single examples from many sites. At Beauport Park, where there are at least 25 examples, it is interesting to note that these are confined to tiles which carry one type of CL BR stamp (Brodribb type 20). This suggests that the stamper was the same man who made the cut-aways, and is a useful piece of evidence of tile-making procedure.

The cut-away at the bottom end of the flange tends to be longer than the top cut-away and can be as long as 10 cm. Its purpose is to reduce the width so that the tile can slot into the part cut-away at the top of the *tegula* set below it on the roof. This reduction of width can be made in several ways. (Fig. 7)

Easily the commonest is type 1, which is found on some 75 per cent of all *tegulae*. The rarest is type 3 which is quite different in that each of the bottom corners of the *tegula* has been knocked off *after* firing in an effort to make the tile fit with the one below.

Cut-aways both top and bottom are usually sharp edged and the knife mark is often visible. On a few occasions however the top cut-away is imperfect. In certain examples the portion of flange removed has been, in differing ways, only partly cut away: while in other examples the cut-aways have been crudely scooped away with the thumb. All imperfect cut-aways at the top end of the flange would surely make it impossible for the *tegula* above to slot in properly, and sit flush on the surface.

The most unusual set of cut-aways are those on a number of complete *tegulae* from Havant. All the cut-aways on the left-hand side are of the usual type 1, and all those on the right-hand side are of type 4. Some difficulty, perhaps left-handedness, prevented the tile-maker from treating each side in the same way. All these tiles carry the same signature.

Other examples of different types of cut-away on the same tile come from Boulogne and Garden Hill, while a Lapworth one is odd in that it has a perfect cut-away on one side, and none at all on the other. A London *tegula* exceeds this in that it has no cut away on either side, which suggests it could have been used only on the bottom course. Another example from London is unusual in that the cut-away (of type 4) is too narrow to be of any use.

7 *Decoration*

It is very rare to find any attempt to decorate *tegulae* by means of incised lines (not to be confused with signatures), or indentations on the flange. The only examples known in Britain are from Ickl-ingham, Suffolk where a few fragments of *tegulae* have either wavy lines or heavily indented pie crust treatment along the top edge of the flange (West & Plouviez, 1976, 101–2).

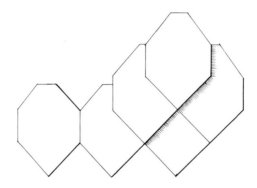

8 Heptagonal roof tiles from Crookhorn

8 *Experimental roofing tiles*

One unusual variety of roofing was the use of unflanged tile, semicircular or pear-shaped, which overlapped each other like the feathers in the tail of a peacock. For this reason Pliny (XXXVI, 44, 159) refers to this arrangement as *pavonacea*. There are many instances found in Britain of such roofing made of angular stone slabs, but only two made of clay tile. These are the heptagonal tiles from the tile kiln at Crookhorn and the pear-shaped tiles from the Roman brickworks at Wykehurst Farm, Cranleigh. The latter resemble the local Horsham stone slab roof-tiles seen today, and they may have been a special order made as a copy of stone tiles. Though the effect may have been pleasing, they were thick and too heavy for the one nail by which they were attached. (Hanworth, 1968, 32 and Goodchild 1937, 93).

Another experiment produced one of the oddest tiles to be found in Britain. From the site at Wendens Ambo, Essex there is a single example, almost complete, of a roofing tile that has on one side the flange of a usual *tegula*, but the other side turns into an *imbrex*.

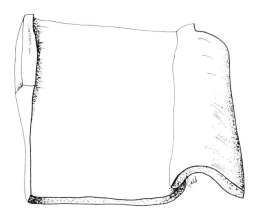

9   Unusual hybrid roof-tile from Wendens Ambo

One very small flanged tile of *tegula* type seems to have no parallel. It comes from Foscott, and is square with lengths of 310 mm, the body thickness is 20 mm and the external depth of the flange is 45 mm. Though the existence of a flange suggests use as a tegula, there are no cut-outs at either top or bottom, and there is no evidence of its provenance or use.

9 (a)   *Tegula with large central hole*

An early example of a *tegula* with a circular hole about 200 mm in diameter comes from a Hellenistic house at Caulonia (5th century BC). The purpose was to let in light and air on a roof or in a passageway, and a raised rim round the hole diverted any water resulting from a shower. It would no doubt be possible to block up the hole during the rainy season (Orsi 1914, 167 and fig. 43). If laid flat on the ridge, it could have carried a chimney pot fitted over the hole.

A partial example of a perforated *tegula* can be seen in the Arelate Museum at Arles. It measured 280 mm in length with an estimated width of 290 mm. The hole was 150 mm in diameter and had an interior depth, including its raised rim, of 60 mm. There is also a fragmentary example at Herculaneum.

Only two examples come from Roman Britain. One comes from Holt and is a fragment 260+ mm wide and at least 200 mm long. There are no cut-aways. A quarter of the circumference of the hole is present, giving an estimated diameter of 210 mm. Round the hole is

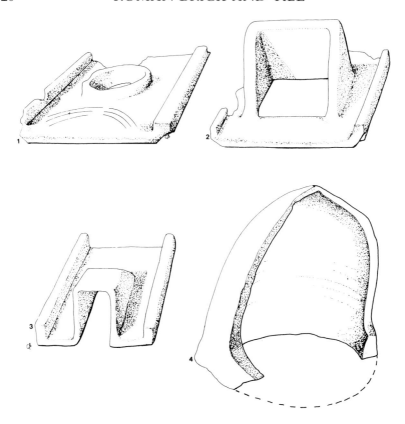

10   Holes and Hoods
    1.   *Tegula* with central hole (after Ludovici). (Scale ⅛)
    2.   *Tegula* with integrated hood. (Scale ⅛)
    3.   Example of hood cut from fron edge. (Scale ⅛)
    4.   Detachable hood from Holt. (Scale ¼)

a rim 45 mm wide, raised 20 mm above the surface of the face, which is 40 mm deep. The other example consists of a quarter of a *tegula* recently found at Colchester; this suggests a hole in the centre with a diameter of about 220 mm. (Pers. comm. Nina Crummy)

9 (b)   *Tegula with an angular hood*

Another variant of *tegula* has a hood attached for the purpose of letting in light or acting as a ventilator. There are two forms: in one the hood is attached over a central cut-out space as figured in a drawing from Ludovici (1912, 193 and fig. 145); in another form the hood is integrated, the whole hooded area being cut back from the front edge of the tile. (Hofmann, 1975, 14).

Similar hoods or vents can be seen today attached to *tegulae* on roofs in Rome, and the practice may have survived from classical times. One example, on the roof of the British School at Rome, was mounted above a hole in the face of the *tegula*, and not integrated into the tile. A hood such as this was found at Holt. It has a diameter of 230 mm, a height of 300 mm, and covers about two-thirds of the circular area, but has lost the rim round the remaining third. It may well have been associated with the perforated *tegula* from Holt mentioned above.

Another example of a roof-tile with the similar purpose of providing a vent or exit hole can be seen in the Musée delle Terme, Rome. Instead of a hood there is a circular pipe 200 mm in diameter projecting from the face of the tile, like a chimney-pot (Middleton, 1892, 123). This would seem to be an example of what appears in the Diocletian Price List as the *auriculatum*, or exit pipe, attached to a hole in the *tegula*. (Erim and Reynolds, 1973, 103)

10   *Other uses of* tegulae

Though originally created for roofing the *tegula* can be used for many other purposes, and like all Roman tile, is readily adaptable. It is used for flooring, bonding courses, foundation courses for walls, capping for *pilae*, hypocaust *pilae*, locker bases, steps, wall cavities, draining, base of hearths, capping for tops of walls, ovens, flue dampers.

11   *Tile tombs and cists*

The finest collection of Romano-British tile tombs, with eight complete examples, can be seen in the Hospitium section of the York museum. These are generally of the inverted V tent-like type, with three or four *tegulae* per side, pitched against one another and the joint at the apex covered by *imbrices* (Wellbeloved, 1842, pl.xi, fig. 27).

Of the many examples from other countries, the Sacellum at Paestum has already been mentioned (p. 5). Elsewhere, at Caulonia in the fifth century BC, tiles were put beneath the corpse and erected over it as 'a *capanna*' to protect it from the pressure of earth. The Locrians also made miniature roofs of specially prepared large curved roof tiles. There were similar finds at Metaponto (Blake 1947, 285).

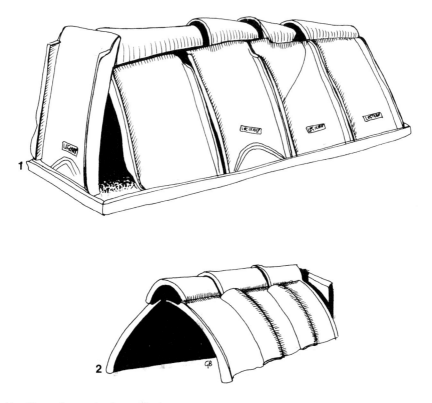

11   Two tile-tombs from York

Tombs found at Strasbourg in 1721 were made of eight *tegulae*, four
on each side, but with no ends or ridge tiles. The *tegulae* carried
stamps of the 8th Legion Augusta (Gough 1786, xxiii).

There is an interesting variation of *tegula* fitting, not found in
Britain, in two tombs at St-Hilaire à Ollières, Var. Each *tegula* has
half the length of its top end cut away to a depth of about 30 mm.
This enables it to fit in with the opposite sloping *tegula* in a close joint
at the apex and then to be covered by an *imbrex*. (Cazzare 1976, pl.1).

IMBREX

Though the *tegula* and *imbrex* can be used independently, they are
more usually found in complementary use. In Diocletian's Edict on

Prices they are found in a tariff of items of building materials (De Fictilibus) (Erim and Reynolds, 1973, 108). They are linked together as a single item, though unfortunately the price in *denarii* is missing from the text. This *'tegula* cum *imbrice'* is listed as one of the best quality (*formae primae*), which possibly suggests that there were various grades of tile available.

Some idea of the *comparative* values of imbrixes and tegulae is given in a passage in Cato's De Agri Cultura, XIV, 4. The *imbrex* (for which Cato uses the old word *vallus*) is to count in value as one quarter of a *tegulae* i.e. four *valli* equal one *tegula*. If this is the correct interpretation of a difficult passage, the *imbrex* seems cheap.

Vitruvius states that in ancient times the idea of an *imbrex* came from the making of ridges of clay to be smeared over the gap between flat sections of roofing (*tecta*) (II, 1, 3). *Imbrices* were used as the earliest type of tiled roofing in Greece in the seventh century BC, the roof being made throughout of concave tiles laid side by side with convex tiles covering the joints (Blake, 1947, 304). This 'over and under' form of roofing is known as the 'Laconian' system, and can still be seen all over the Mediterranean area.

Early Sicilian tiles were not semi-circular, but shallow, and some had a rudimentary flange or raised lip round the edge of the wider end. (Wilson, 1979, 20–22). A similar lip is found on *imbrices* in Britain at Richborough, Griff Hill Farm, Great Casterton, and Caistor by Norwich.

Classical references to the *imbrex* by itself are rare, though Virgil refers to a hut being covered *'imbrice'* (Georgics, IV, 296). There are

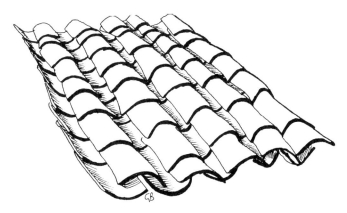

12   Example of Laconian system of roofing

one or two odd formations based upon the word *imbrex*. Lugli refers to '*tegulae imbricatae*' (1957, 547), while Sidonius Apollinaris (Epistles II, 2, 5) mentions '*dorsa tegulis interjacentibus imbricarentur*'. Pliny refers to the surface on shellfish as '*imbricatim undata*' (corrugated like tiles) (IX, 52, 103). Suetonius makes further use of the word in his story of the way in which the Emperor Nero arranged three special claques to applaud his performances. These had learnt the Alexandrine methods and were known as *BOMBOS, IMBRICES,* and *TESTAS.* This would seem to refer to the noises created by the buzzing of bees, rain drumming on the roof, and the clanging together of bricks or pots. (Nero, 20) Isidorus, Bishop of Hispalis AD 600–636, makes a clear statement about the purpose of an *imbrex*: 'Tegulae quae tegunt aedes et imbrices quod accipiunt imbres' (Orig. XV, 8). The connection between *imber*: a shower of rain, and the word *imbrex* is patent.

On the rare occasions when archaeological reports of the past refer to tile and brick, the *imbrex* is sometimes made obscure by being referred to in a variety of terms, e.g. curved tile, cover tile, gutter tile, joint tile, rounded, semicircular or ridge tile. Information about the *imbrex* is not so extensive as for the *tegula* because from all sites there are usually fewer examples of *imbrex*. In the survey 330 complete *imbrices* were listed compared with 613 complete *tegulae*. One reason for this is because *imbrices* are not needed on the outside edges of a gabled roof. Another reason is that not all *tegulae* found on a site may have come from the roof, but may have had other uses. The total number of *imbrices* required also depends upon the amount of overlap. There is some slight evidence about this: two *imbrices* from Nottingham have clear traces of mortar extending for 50 mm on the outside of the narrower end, while another, has the same traces covering 50 mm on the underside of the wider end, i.e. there was an overlap of 50 mm when the two tiles were set together.

From Exeter there is part of an *imbrex* which has a coating of mortar adhering across the whole area of the inside of the wider end to the length of 75 mm. There is similar evidence from Silchester, and also from Quinton, which has an *imbrex* with a patch of mortar underneath the wide end which extends for 90 mm.

Decorative features exist on some *imbrices*, though they are rare. There are several varieties of these features and they cannot all be regarded as aids for keying to mortar.

1   *Ribbed lines or runnels along the length of the crest*

Seventeen sites have produced *imbrices* which have two or three finger-made lines running the whole length of the tile. Others have similar lines covering the whole surface.

2   Lines across the gable at the wider end

There are examples which carry a series of finger-made straight lines running directly over the gable from edge to edge or formed in a squiggle. In other examples from seven sites lines in a similar position have been put on with a comb.

3   Signatures

From Beauport Park all but one of the 56 complete *imbrices* carry either a CL BR stamp or a signature mark similar to that found on *tegulae*. This usually occurs on the right-hand side of the gable near the wider end. A few other sites have produced *imbrices* with signatures in this position, some of them combed.

4   Decoration

There are two fragmentary examples from Cirencester of elaborate decoration: one shows an animal, the other a human figure. (McWhirr & Viner 197, 362 and fig. 2). A different form of decoration has been found at Icklingham: one complete *imbrex* has a raised keel or midriff bifurcating at the lower end; fifteen other fragments have frilled edges or grooved patterns. (West and Plouviez, 1976, 101) (fig. 44, 97 a,b,c & 102)

5   Stamps

Seventy stamps have been found on complete *imbrices*, all but four coming from the Classis Britannica.

6   Unofficial imprints

The animal impressions so often found on tiles are very rare on *imbrices*. One example from Beauport Park has a dog print which has torn away the edge on an *imbrex* as though the dog had reached up to a tile drying on a raised rack. Dog prints from other sites support this theory.

There are a number of deep finger marks found under the middle of the side edge of *imbrices*, made when the tile was being carried at the point of balance.

7 *Holes*

It is rare to find any form of hole on an *imbrex*. An example from Springhead has the surface pitted with superficial holes made apparently with a stick; one from York has a hole on top of the crest, but it does not go right through, while another has a completely penetrating hole. A Frilford *imbrex* has one hole right through as well as four others penetrating only half way; one from Reculver has a spike hole in one edge.

8 *Size*

The average length of the complete *imbrices* studied is 398 mm, ranging from 510 mm (Chester) and 500 mm (Holt and York) down to 360 mm (Icklingham). There is nothing to approach the size of an *imbrex* in the Musée at Orange: it is 67 mm long, had little taper and map possibly have been made for a drain or for use on the ridge.

The average width at the wider end is 176.2 mm and ranges from 220 mm (Crookhorn and York) to as little as 130 mm (Brading, Dursley, and Havant). The average width at the narrower end is 135.1 mm. Measurement is sometimes made difficult when the corners have either splayed out (e.g. Boulogne examples) or been pinched inwards.

The average overall height at the wider end is 93 mm with the narrower end 20 mm less. The thickness averages 20 mm, with a range from 30 mm to 14 mm. Longer *imbrices* are not necessarily thicker.

Eight sites have produced examples of *imbrices* having the whole edge of the narrower end chamfered off in order to provide an easier fit for the overlap. Some sites have produced several varieties of *imbrex*: Beauport Park, for example, uses types of three different lengths.

As with the *tegula*, the *imbrex* can be used in many ways: Springhead had a series of pipes resting in a bed made of *imbrices*. There are examples from Norton Disney, Folkestone, Brecon, Towcester and no doubt many other sites where the *imbrex* has been used directly as a drain. At Castlefield a hearth was created by a series of inverted *imbrices*; at Rockbourne in Room xxix the *pilae* of a hypocaust were made by cementing two *imbrices* together; while at Verulamium *imbrices* were used in pairs as draining channels in the foundation of a hypocaust. At Beauport Park in three rooms, and Verulamium (Room 18) *imbrices* were used as makeshift flues instead of the usual box-tiles, and *imbrices* must often have been used as ridge tiles on the roof.

RIDGE TILE, and other curved tile

A third type of tile associated with roofing is the ridge tile, whose purpose was to cover the gap where the *tegulae* meet at the apex of the roof. Though the *imbrex* was no doubt often used for this, special tiles were sometimes made, and Blake (1947, 7) quotes early examples from Italy. Nothing so elaborate seems to have been used for the covering of the ridges of roof in Britain. The common practice seems to be the use of ordinary *imbrices* either butted together or overlapping in what would have created a jagged skyline.

There are however several examples of specially made ridge-tile resembling an *imbrex*, but which had little taper and were generally thicker. The sites producing these examples are:

1 LITTLECOTE One example is 420 mm long (cf the *sesquipedalis*), has a base width of 330 mm, a height of 130 mm, an arc of 420 mm and a thickness of 27 mm. There is some faint combing, and a 'cross' signature. The roofing tiles were of stone.
2 ALCESTER There is one example 310 mm long and 170 mm wide. The crest is flattened and the external surface heavily frosted except for a distance of 50 mm from the end, which remains dark red in colour and was obviously a section covered by overlap. The roofing tiles were of stone.
3 SPARSHOLT Many fragments of a semicircular tile were found with a span of 280 to 320 mm, a length of at least 310 mm, and a thickness of 30 mm. The height was 90 mm. The surface has several combed lines, some straight, some squiggles made by a six-tooth comb giving a track of 25 mm. Roofing tiles made of stone.
4 NEWPORT I.O.W. Several fragments belong to a curved tile which has a base width estimated by Tomalin at 220 mm (1975, 13). The length is unknown, but the thickness is 25 mm. At one end of the crest are groups of one, two, or three impressions made by finger-tips, and the finger-nail scratch can be seen. These marks may represent personal signatures, or possibly 'tally-marks', and they are unique. The roofing tiles amongst which these fragments were found were made of stone.

It is interesting to note that these examples of capping for the ridge were all found in close association with fallen roof tiles made of stone rather than of baked clay.

None of the examples just quoted give any evidence for ridge tiles on a roof covered with *tegulae*, and there is only one alleged example of this, though it has no provenance to show its connection with any particular roof. This is a tile from Holt which was reported on as a 'Ridge Tile: One example, length 19 inches for covering joints of *tegulae* at the summit of the roof. The width is the same throughout and the section truly semicircular, while the *imbrex* increases in width from top to bottom, and is more triangular in section.' (Grimes, 1930, 135) It has been recently measured at 550 mm (which is 21¾ inches) and is 190 mm wide. There is no taper. The height is 130 mm, and the thickness only 17 mm, which is less than most *imbrices*. It differs from the usual *imbrex* found at Holt, which is 500 mm long and stands 110 mm high.

A tile without taper could easily be butted to the next one in a simple joint, but the attested Ridge tiles from roofs with stone tiles tended to have some taper, and the one from Alcester gives real evidence of overlap.

Other possible sources of evidence as to how the ridges were covered could come from representations of roofs shown on sarcophagi (e.g. the Simpelfeld example from Leyden: see Brogan, 1953, fig. 49), but it is not easy to see from these exactly what was done.

There are three other complete examples of a curved tile which is different from the usual *imbrex* in thickness and in curve, and these may well be genuine ridge tiles. The one from Winchester measures 425 mm long, is 260–300 mm wide, and 140 mm tall at the wider end, which has combing over the crest. There is no provenance, but as it is in the Winchester Museum, it may have come from a locality that used stone tiles, like Sparsholt, which is not far away. Of the other complete tiles one comes from the unprovenanced collection (probably London) at the British Museum store; it is 500 mm long, 235 mm wide, and stands only 80 mm high. The other comes from Brantingham. It is a perfect example 340 mm long and 260 mm wide with no taper. It stands 160 mm tall and is 30 mm thick.

There are several fragments of what seems to be tile of the same type; one comes from Cirencester and another example from Charterhouse Mendip.

To revert to Grimes' remark about the truly semicircular tile being suitable for a ridge tile: there are several examples of such curved tile which could under this criterion be possible examples of ridge tile, but they are all small and quite unlike the ridge tiles so far mentioned. They come from Copdock (300 mm long, 100 mm wide, and 95 mm high), from Brading (300 mm long, 130 mm wide, and 75 mm tall) and from Brixworth and Beauport Park (340 mm long, 130 mm wide, and 80 mm tall). All these are about a Roman foot long, and may be drains.

The setting of the roof tiles on the British School at Rome, as well as some of the buildings attached to the Museo delle Terme Diocleziano, provide an alternative form of ridge capping. The rafters, where the *tegulae* converge towards the apex, have been cut off, leaving a flat area; this was capped by *tegulae* and across the raised flanges of these flat capping *tegulae imbrices* were laid. If this particular setting of tiles on a roof can be seen in present times, might not the Romans have treated their roofs in the past in the same way? In our attempts to learn the practices of the ancients, we tend to forget that there are many ways of doing things, each subject to changes of time and place, and even fashion.

ANTEFIX

The Greeks originated the idea of attaching to the end of the lowest course of *imbrices* on the roof a ceramic ornament known now as an antefix. This would not only fill a space, but would protect any exposed woodwork, and provide decoration. There were also other ceramic attachments in the form of cresting, revetment plaques, acroteria, simae, gutters and water spouts. The subject is admirably covered by Blagg (1979, 267–384).

The Romans continued the tradition. Livy refers to lightning bringing down statues that stood 'in antefixis fictilibus' (Hist. XXVI, 23, 5) and he also stated that 'too many laugh at the fictile antefixes of our Roman gods' (Hist. XXXIV, 4, 4)

Antefixes found in Roman Britain have been fully discussed. (Toynbee, 1964, 428–431). The face of the antefix is basically triangular or pentagonal, and at the back there is often a projection that can plug into the wider end of the *imbrex*, but some have a semicircular integral extension of *imbrex* shape that can be abutted to an *imbrex*.

There is an antefix from Chester which shows how the face was luted on to a block that ended in *imbrex* shape. The face had broken away from the block at the join, and deep score marks can be seen that were made to help make a good attachment.

On some large buildings in Athens, and also on the roof of the

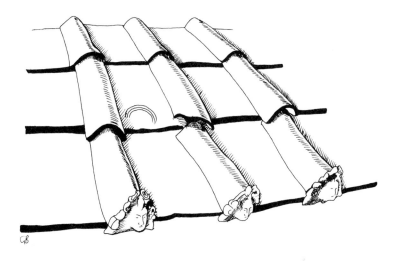

13   The setting of ante-fixes at the edge of roof

14   Various types of antefix
     a. Holt (Scale ¼);   b. Chester;   c. Silchester (Scale ⅛);   (d) Italy

Museum at Olympia, a modern form of antefix can be seen, set at the bottom of every course of *imbrices*, creating a serried line. This might give some indication of the way in which they were set in ancient times, but Romano-British sites have produced nothing like enough examples to provide evidence that they were set all along the eaves. An alternative is that they were placed intermittently, and especially at corners, or were confined to a position at the top of each gable, set at the end of the ridge.

The angle of the face presented to view does not seem to be constant. If the face is mounted at right angles to the base it would be seen as upright when set at the ridge-ends. If the same was set at the end of the *imbrices* on the eaves, then the face would lean forward.

The pictorial designs on antefixes vary considerably. Of the seven types found at Holt, six display the letters LEG XX, as well as the boar, the legionary badge. Other legions displayed their badge in the same way, e.g. the Lion of Legion XVI at Neuss. The seventh design from Holt has a motif with a 'magical' significance to protect the inmates from evil influences. Designs from Caerleon had a similar purpose. Some modern houses built in Greece still have antefixes (some made of cement), and these probably have some element of apotropaic purpose. There is also a slight analogy with the English custom of nailing up a horseshoe for good luck.

'CHIMNEY POT'

There is another form of ceramic roof accessory which often takes the shape of a tapering cylinder. It has been found on some thirty-five sites in Britain, but only ten examples have been at all complete; the tallest comes from Beauport Park, and stands 47 cm high with a round open base 21 cm in diameter.

The majority of these objects are reported in a posthumous paper by A. W. G. Lowther (1976, 35–48). Many resemble a small pharos built in tiers with triangular window-like vents; they would appear to make excellent chimney pots, and the present writer has seen just such an object in use on a roof of a house in the old city of Ragusa (Dubrovnik).

One difficulty is that with the exception of two examples which are actually integrated into curved ridge tiles there is no evidence of the 'pots' having come off a roof. All the others could have stood on the ridge only if it was formed of *tegulae* laid flat possibly with a central hole over which the pot could be set.

15   1. Chimney integrated with ridge-tile – Norton. (Scale ⅛)
     2. Chimney pot – Beauport Park. (Scale ⅛)

One of the two examples comes from Norton, E. Yorkshire,
where in 1954 a complete example of 'chimney-pot' was found : it
had been built into a tapering *imbrex*-shaped tile, which was 220 mm
long, with a span of 150 mm. The roof tiles were made of slate.
(Lowther, 1976, 38, pl.11 and fig. 3). The other similar example
comes from Silchester. Neither the pot nor the curved tile to which it
is attached is complete, but the length of the fragment is 200 mm.
(Lowther, *ibid*, 46) These two integrated pots leave no doubt as to
their purpose of providing a vent for smoke or hot air.

It may be surmised that fumes from the vertical box-flues could
have emerged into a roof space sealed from the rooms below, and
from there come out through a chimney. There is rare evidence from
Verulamium of a roller-printed box-flue tile with a plain extension
which could have projected through the ceiling, possibly to support
a roof mounted ventilator (Wilson, 1984, 113, fig. 50 (18)). We could
be more certain about the exact purpose of such pots if we had some
evidence of them shown *in situ*, but such information is confined
either to Roman wall paintings which are more usually impressions
than representations, or to mosaics which are equally indefinite.
Among the most interesting of these is a mosaic (now lost) of a large

Roman house at Oued-Atmenia in Algeria; fortunately there is a reproduction of it, and this shows several chimney-pots. (Graham, 1886, 125 ff, and fig. 177)

Perhaps, like so many other ceramic items, there could have been other uses. Suggestions for these include the covering of lamps (giving a lantern effect), a covering for the burning of aromatics, or simply for ventilation.

CHAPTER 2

BRICKS

Bessalis

The main function of this small square brick was to create *pilae* (pillars or piers) to support the *suspensura*, i.e. the floor suspended above the hypocaust. Vitruvius (V.10.2) refers to this brick used for the *pilae* as 'laterculus besalis' with a single 's', but 'ss' is more usually found. The word *bes* basically means 'two-thirds of a unit', and the unit concerned here is the Roman foot (*pes*) which measured 12 Roman inches (*unciae*), or 11.64 English inches. An *uncia* really means 'one twelfth of anything'. Two-thirds of a Roman foot came to eight inches, and there is an adjective *'bessalis'* from the word *'bes'* which means 'comprising the number eight'. This is why Vitruvius uses the term 'laterculus besalis' to mean a little eight inch brick.

The average length (and width) of 608 recorded complete *bessales* (this excludes any still *in situ*) works out at 7.8 Roman inches (*unciae*) which is the equivalent of 198 mm, and this satisfactorily confirms Vitruvius' statement. The measurements of these complete *bessales* range from 235 mm (a London example) to 170 mm (London and Darenth). There is also variation in thickness: the average is 43 mm (which is a fifth of the width), but the range differs from 90 mm (Godmanchester) to 25 mm (Atworth). The Godmanchester *bessalis* is exceptional, and is 30 mm thicker than the next thickest example of 60 mm.

Though there is little dictionary evidence for the word *Pilaris* (as opposed to *Pĭlaris* meaning 'connected with *pila*: a ball'), it seems possible that this word could be an adjective concerned with *pila* in the context of a pillar of a hypocaust. The sole evidence comes from a graffito on a tile from Wiggonholt which reads:

PI (LARES . . .) XX
CVNIATI IIII
TVBV (LI) N DLX

and seems to refer to the making of at least twenty pillar tiles, four voussoirs, and 560 box-flue tiles (Winbolt and Goodchild, 1940 66–7, and Tomlin, 1979, 23). The graffito seems to refer to a batch total, and Winbolt calculates that some 540 box-flue tiles would have been required for the building, which comes close to the 560 mentioned. Though this evidence for the word *pilaris* as an alternative for *bessalis* is so slight, it seems reasonable to suppose that such a word existed, and such a technical term might well escape survival in literary evidence.

There is a variant form of *bessalis* in which the brick is round instead of square, but with the same diameter. Twenty-three different sites use these round *bessales*, and it would seem that they were usually used to form *pilae*. At Listercombe the hypocaust was formed by alternate square and round *pilae* (Rudder, 1800, 334) and at Silchester in Room I there were seven rows of *pilae* standing 3 feet 4 inches tall, four of which were square and three were circular (Price, 1887, 273). Also at Silchester there was a composite hypocaust with its centre made of 24 close-set *pilae*, all of which were made of octagonal *bessales* standing at least 11 tiles tall.

There is evidence from overseas of examples of circular *bessales* with holes in the centre from Pompeii and Piazza Armerina (Wilson, 1979, 33 n.5). The only comparative example from Roman Britain of central holes seems to be the three square *bessales*, measuring 230 mm across and 60 mm deep, found at Chester: these have a square central hole of 60 × 60 mm.

Bessales are not always exactly square, and the oddest mis–shape is an example from Fiddler's Hamlet, in which 3 sides measure 210 mm and the other side only 190 mm.

Like other forms of Roman brick and tile the *bessalis* had other uses apart from its prime function as maker of *pilae*. These include flooring, archways, and bonding.

One building form common elsewhere but not in Britain was the use of triangular brick laid in mortar with the long edge to form a facing for a wall. In Italy *bessales* normally 197 mm square were 'for the most part made to furnish triangular bricks for wall facing'. (Blake, 1959, 164) They were cheap to make and could easily be formed into a triangle by a skilled blow of the hammer. This use became the standard practice for facing brick.

Of the 608 examples of *bessales* only 54 (9%) have been 'signed' with some mark, and it may be that such a simple form of brick was not generally considered worthy of signature. Stamps are rare; even at Beauport Park which has produced 72 complete *bessales*, and where the practice of stamping seems so common, there is not a single example of a complete stamped *bessalis*, though there is one stamp on a partial *bessalis*.

There are however 12 examples of *bessales* which carry a tally-mark: six from Beauport Park, five from Cranbrook, and one from Folkestone. These are all Classis Britannica sites.

Pedalis

Since the Roman *pes* seems to have been the basic unit for all sizes of brick and tile, it is not surprising that there is a brick that measures exactly one square foot. Its chief function was to act as capping or base brick for *pilae* made of the smaller *bessales*. There are few classical references to the *pedalis*, but in the section 'De Fictilibus' in Diocletian's Edict on Maximum Prices, one item is listed as 'laterem puda (l) em', (for 'pedalem') and priced at four *denarii*.

Vitruvius (II, 3, 3) and later Pliny, who copied him almost word for word, listed three types of tile known to the Greeks: the *lydion*, the *pentadoron*, and the *tetradoron*, but both state that the only one used by 'us' (i.e. the Romans) was the lydion which measured 1 foot 6 inches by 1 foot.

The word *tetradoron*, as explained by Pliny (XXXV, 49, 171), means 'having a width of four palms', and since according to Hultsch (1882, 1971 ed., 700) a *palmus* measured the equivalent of 739 mm, thus four *palmi* came to 295 mm, which exactly equals one Roman *pes* (11.64 inches). It is possible that the reason for Vitruvius not regarding this as a Roman tile was that the *tetradoron/pedalis* (like other types of tile not mentioned by Vitruvius) was not in general use at the time Vitruvius was writing.

Complete examples of *pedales* are rare, and the survey recorded only 200. These have an average size of 281 mm square, which is just under the Roman foot. Many of them are not quite square: one from Stonham Aspal measures 345 mm × 240 mm, Eccles has one of 340 mm × 290 mm and Sparsholt one of 330 mm × 295 mm. These may be tiles made for a special purpose.

The average thickness of the *pedalis* is 46 mm, which is thicker than that of the *bessalis*. The thickness varies from 25 mm (Silchester) to 70 mm (also Silchester). Compared with the *bessalis* a greater quantity carry signatures, 31 out of 83 (37 per cent); eight have stamps (six with CL BR, and two with PP.BR.LON). No tally marks have been found.

The reason for the shortage of complete examples may be that when acting as caps for the *pilae* most were smashed up when the hypocaust collapsed, while others, acting as bases for *pilae* that still stand *in situ*, have not been recorded.

Among other possible uses of the *pedalis*, there are several examples of its use to make a hearth, as recorded from Newport (IOW), Pevensey and Watercrook.

Lydion

The word *lydium* has an obvious connection with Lydia in Asia, and by transference it also comes to have the meaning 'Etruscan'. This brick is one of the commonest of those used by Romans, and since there is no official word for it let us follow Vitruvius and refer to it as the Lydian brick, or simply as 'Lydion'. According to Davey, who also names it as Lydion, this brick may have had its prototype in a much earlier Minoan brick which was the same size in plan, but was twice as thick (1961, 72).

Three almost complete examples of *Lydion* measuring 44 cm × 29 cm × 14 cm were found at Arezzo in excavations between 1910–1918 on the ancient city wall which Vitruvius himself had mentioned with admiration (Vit. II, 8, 9). These examples had an extreme thickness recalling the old Minoan brick; the dimensions may have been brought by the Etruscans from their original homeland (Blake, 1947, 279).

The *Lydion* was most suitable for bonding or lacing courses found in the walls of large public buildings or defences. The purpose of these courses was twofold: when the mason building the wall found that he had reached the limit for comfortable working, a course of brick was put on to provide a new level base. Then staging was set up and the mason could proceed with his work. Posts concerned with the scaffolding or with the business of keeping the walls vertical sometimes had their heads socketed into the actual wall, leaving holes as much as 9 inches deep; these put-log holes sometimes are seen, e.g. at Lympne, and in the city walls of Caerwent.

These holes must not be confused with small circular holes (voids) some 2½ inches (63 mm) to 4 inches (102 mm) in diameter that go right through the masonry as can be seen at Verulamium, Caernarvon, Caer Gypi (Holyhead), and Lympne. These horizontal holes were for rods placed intermittently to bind together the staging from

16   Tile courses in wall, Verulamium

which the builder worked, or possibly the boarding used in the construction of the walls (Wheeler, 1932, 121–2).

The second function of the brick courses was to bind together the face and the core, especially when the cement was still soft. Even the thickest of walls had only thin outer skins of dressed masonry, the interior being filled in with loose small stone mixed with concrete. To be wholly effective the lacing course had to extend over the full width of the wall, though sometimes the course goes along only the outer part of the wall, as can be seen clearly in a broken section of the walls at Pevensey Castle.

Two of the highest standing examples of wall in Roman Britain, the Jewry wall at Leicester, and the 'Old Work' at Wroxeter, give a good picture of the differing intervals between courses, and the number of rows in each course. The overall depth of any course depends not only upon the number of rows of tile used, but also upon the depth of the tile itself, and the width of the mortar joints. It was most important that the top rows should be level, and irregularities caused by the scrap tile sometimes used could be adjusted by the thickness of mortar. Generally speaking the tendency in Rome was for the mortar joints to increase in thickness as time went on, and in Britain the same practice was followed, e.g. the joints of brick courses in the earlier walls of London, Colchester, and Verulamium range from ½ inch to 1½ inches, and are very regular, while the joints to be seen in the later Saxon Shore defences are not only rougher, but sometimes amount to 3 inches or more in thickness. This is an example, to quote Wheeler, of the 'tendency in the late work of Roman Britain to emphasise the importance of the concrete or mortar at the expense of the other material' (1932, 133).

A most informative account of lacing courses comes from Wheeler in his description of the city wall at Verulamium:

The average section of the wall shows above the footings a double brick lacing-course running completely through the structure, surmounted by a third course of bricks restricted to the facing only, the three courses of bricks being recessed successively to form the total external scarcement of 11 inches. The bricks average 1 ft 4½ in by 11½ in by 1½ in. Above these brick courses the wall is carried up in flint for a further height of 2 ft 9 in, the facing flints being sliced in the better-built portions. Above this a triple lacing-course running through the wall and surmounted by a further 2 ft 4 in of flint-work. There follows a double or triple lacing-course and another 2 ft 9 in or 3 ft of flint-work, with yet another double lacing-course above. The maximum surviving height of the wall above the footings is 12 ft 6 in, but there is no evidence as to the original total dimensions. (Wheeler and Wheeler, 1936, 59).

This may suggest that bonding courses were usually made of *Lydion*, but though this was the most suitable brick for the job, other forms of bricks were also used. There are also examples of how useful *Lydion* could be in some of the internal walls such as at Wroxeter where three *Lydion* bricks, set side by side, with the longer edge exposed, create the full width of the wall (about 900 mm).

Lydion brick was also good for flooring, e.g. at Wroxeter (Leighton, 1789, 325), and could be used for the capping of *pilae* as an alternative for *pedalis* brick (Davey, 1961, 197, fig. 108).

There are several ways in which bricks can be keyed into the mortar bed. A Ribchester brick is heavily scored on the top side; but a more effective way than scoring was the setting of blobs of clay on the top surface of the brick which could not only bed down into the mortar, but would also prevent the mortar from squashing out under the weight of the brick. This treatment of brick with bosses of clay is fully discussed under the section *Tegula Mammata* (Type A). Another help to bonding has been found occasionally in the chamfering off at 45 degrees for a distance of about 50 mm of one of the shorter sides. The placing together of two of these chamfered bricks would provide a better joint.

Examples of this chamfering are rare, and have been found only at Fishbourne, Colchester, Exeter, Silksted, Caerleon, Leicester, and Silchester. From Fishbourne and Silchester come unusual examples of *Lydion* brick which are not only chamfered, but also have bosses attached to the top surface.

There are 314 examples of complete *Lydion* giving an average size of 403 mm × 280 mm × 41 mm deep. The size of individual items ranges from one of 480 mm × 310 mm (London) to one of 335 mm × 230 mm (Caister). The thickness ranges from 70 mm (Wroxeter) and 65 mm (Verulamium and Alfoldean) down to 25 mm (Caistor). Of the 314 listed items 47 have *mammae* in various formation (15.0 per cent), 81 have signatures (25.7 per cent), 23 have impressions of foot/shoe or animal (7.3 per cent), and 8 carry stamps (2.5 per cent).

Sesquipedalis

There are few classical references to the brick named *sesquipedalis* which had a measurement of 1½ feet square (443 mm). Vitruvius mentions the *tegula sesquipedalis* as suitable brick to make a pavement on which to mount the *pilae* of the hypocaust (V.10.2). Other references include one to 'tegl. secipedale' (CIL XV, 650). They could also be used as flooring, and can be seen in arches in Ostia and in Rome.

The survey revealed 42 complete and 10 partial examples coming from 26 sites. The average size is 406 mm. The largest example of 460 mm comes from London and the smallest, from Shakenoak, is of 350 mm. The average thickness is 52 mm ranging from 70 mm down to 40 mm.

Among the few to be found *in situ* are seven examples from Beauport Park, and they all formed parts of floors. Three of them have a *mamma* attached near each corner, and the bricks were laid facing downwards so that the *mammae* would act as keys into the mortar into which they were bedded.

Of the examples listed, seventeen have signatures, three have animal impressions, and five have stamps.

Tegula bipedalis

The *bipedalis* is the largest of all Roman bricks and measures 2 feet square, (5914 mm); it has many different uses and is more versatile than the *sesquipedalis*. Vitruvius names the *bipedalis* and its functions more frequently than any other brick. One use was to bridge the gaps between the *pilae* of the hypocaust, and thus form the basis of the *suspensura* (V, 10, 2). He may possibly include *bipedales* among the 'tegulae sine marginibus' which he refers to as being slung on iron hooks just below the wooden joists which formed a vaulted roof. This would protect the joists from being rotted by steam from the bath below (V, 10, 3).

Reference to the *bipedalis* brick comes occasionally in inscriptions, e.g. 'tegl bipedal' (CIL XV, 651), 'bipedale' and 'bip' (both without the word *tegula*) in CIL XV 362 and 532 (a brick stamp) respectively. Palladius uses the form *bipeda* to mean a 2 foot square brick (Opus Agri. I, 19, i). The Diocletian Edict (Ch.7, 15) uses the term 'lateres pedum binum' in connection with payments to brick makers.

Other uses of *bipedales* include that of bonding course brick, though the practice of using whole *bipedales* is seldom found before the time of Domitian, (Blake, 1959, 162). From use in flat bonding to use in arches was an obvious step, and the practice of introducing the occasional complete *bipedalis* into an arch made mostly of partial ones served to bind the facing to the core.

As already stated by Vitruvius, *bipedales* were very suitable for bridging the gaps at the top of the pillars of a hypocaust, but not many examples of these have been found *in situ* in Britain. At Beauport Park however they have been found in several rooms bridging over the area where the mouths of channels of a hypocaust meet, and on the same site two other *bipedales* are found in separate places as bonders or quoins at corners of the building.

It might be imagined that *bipedales* by their very size would be most suitable for facing direct on to a wall surface where simple revetment rather than the creation of a space for insulation was required. There are not many examples of this: but at Holt it was necessary to face the walls below ground level on one side of a hypocaust (Grimes, 1930, fig.10), and at Gelligaer, when the level of a hypocaust had to be raised, *bipedales* were set against the walls so that the edge could provide a ledge for the new *suspensura* (Ward, 1909, 51 and fig.8).

The two examples from Holt have nail holes near the corners, and one has a centre hole as well. It is stated that some *bipedales* found at Chester in positions above the hypocaust had perforations which were holes made 'to admit steam into the chamber above': but since these large bricks with holes were resting on the capping above the *pilae*, and in any case had a considerable layer of cement laid on top of them, no vapour or fumes could have penetrated, nor would it have been in the least desirable for them to do so.

On the other hand, in a kiln where hot air was encouraged to circulate the floor might well have needed holes in it to allow the heat to penetrate from below. Perhaps those *bipedales* with holes were originally created for that purpose. Another possibility is that holes, especially those made at random and apparently with a stick, were inserted in order to assist with the firing and to prevent hot gases building up towards explosion, e.g. a *bipedalis* from Beauport Park.

Many *bipedales* are heavily combed, for instance in the Pharos at Dover, and this may simply be to provide keying for such a large object that needed a great amount of mortar.

Examples of complete *bipedales* in Britain are rare, and there are only 23 in the survey, though there are 17 other examples of partial *bipedales* which provide a measurement. The average size was 577 mm square, and the average thickness was 60 mm. The three largest on the list are:

Exeter	600 mm × 600 mm × 80 mm	0.028 cubic m
Dover	595 mm × 595 mm × 75 mm	0.026 cubic m

Langley   610 mm × 610 mm × 70 mm   0.026 cubic m

There is also a partial *bipedalis* from Springhead which measures 610 mm × 390 mm × 85 mm; if this had been a complete square it would probably have surpassed all others with a volume of 0.31 cubic m.

All *bipedales* were extremely heavy, and the Springhead example, when complete, could have had a weight estimated at 139 lbs (63 kg). This would be the equivalent of the combined weight of 11 average *tegulae*. Even this, however, does not compare with some *bipedales* from Fréjus which measure 750 mm × 750 mm × 75 mm, giving a volume of 0.042 cubic m, and an estimated weight of 186 lbs (83 kg). Another measures 1.05 m (Lanciani, 1897, 39).

Many fragments of very thick brick have been found, and it is likely that most examples which are 70 mm or more thick have come from a *bipedalis*. There have however been examples of much smaller brick that have had great thickness, e.g. a *bessalis* from Godman-chester measuring 210 mm × 190 mm × 90 mm. The thickest item noted is a fragment from Chignall St James, which measures 360 mm × 200 mm, and is as much as 100 mm (4 inches) thick. Other thick examples come from Godmanchester, Chichester, Ribchester, and Wanborough – all of which measure about 90 mm thick. These may be the thickest bricks found in Britain, but in Sicily at Taormina bricks have been found as much as 120 mm thick (Blake, 1947, 283).

Features visible on the 40 examples of *bipedales* (including partial ones) are: six stamps, fourteen signatures, four foot/shoe or animal impressions, and nine examples of *tegula mammata* treatment.

Cuneatus (Solid Voussoir)

It is possible to make curved arches with any size of flat brick from *bessales* to *bipedales* simply by adjusting the amount of mortar to induce the curve. It is, however, more satisfactory to create the curve by using brick which is tapered and thus leaves the thickness of the mortar constant. Any wedge-shaped object of stone or brick made to help the formation of an arch, e.g. a keystone, is usually referred to by the French word *voussoir*. Latin has no specific equivalent and when Vitruvius talks of relieving the weight of walling by use of arches with voussoirs, the word he uses is '*cuneus*' which means a wedge (VI, 8, 3).

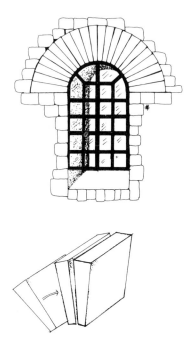

17   Arch made of solid tapering *cuneati*

There are two varieties of voussoir: the solid ones and those similar to the ordinary box-flue, except for being open-sided and having a taper. Since there is no definite Latin term the word *cuneatus* is used here to refer to solid voussoir and *tubulus cuneatus* for the hollow ones. The previously mentioned graffito from Wiggonholt (p. 34) gives what seems to be a short list of types and quantities of tile either made or required for a particular job.

The survey showed that there are 62 examples of *cuneati* from 20 different sites; there are also fourteen partial examples, from seven other sites. The examples fall into several groups, 400 mm × 400 mm, 400 mm × 300 mm, 400 mm × 150 mm; 300 mm × 300 mm and 300 mm × 150 mm. These sizes seem to follow the usual standard forms of 1 foot 6 inches, 1 foot, and introduce the 6 inch measure.

The longest example of 465 mm comes from Ribchester. The thickness of taper ranges from 62 mm at the top to 39 mm at the bottom, a different of 23 mm. The two thickest examples, each

18   Section of wall with flat and semi circular arches, Ostia

measuring 85 mm at the thicker end, are a reused brick from St Augustine's, Canterbury and a similar one from Wroxeter. The thinnest example comes from East Dean, Sussex, it measures 300 mm × 300 mm and tapers from 45 mm to 35 mm.

Of the total 76 examples (complete and partial), twelve carry signatures, and three have stamps.

One voussoir from Wroxeter throws light on the method of production. On one corner of the face at the thinner end is a quarter circle signature which seems to have been cut off sharply, as though it was originally a semicircle cut in half. The depth of this voussoir is 150 mm, so if the brick was originally made at double the size, and then bisected, the mould would have been 300 mm wide – yet again the unit of a Roman *pes*. Two examples from London also have a quarter circle mark like the one from Wroxeter and it may have been cut in the same way.

One characteristic of some solid voussoirs is that both sides are

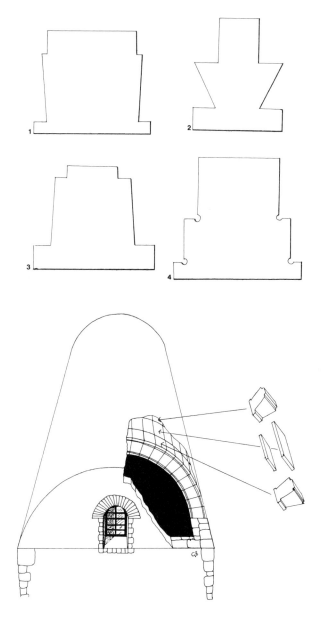

19   Top Four types of solid 'arm-chair' voussoir (Scale ¼)
       1. Bainton;   2. Stanton Low;   3. Ribchester;   4 Leicester. Scale ¼

Bottom Diagram to show the setting of such voussoirs

cleaned off smooth, unlike most brick which shows a smooth topside, and a much rougher underside.

There are a few rare tiles which have central cut-away areas, and because they seem mostly to have some taper in their thickness they are mentioned here.

1   Two complete tiles from Holt are labelled in the report as 'Bridging Tiles' (Grimes, 1930, 19, 136 and fig.9). They measure 320 mm × 305 mm and taper in thickness from 75 mm to 50 mm, and have a square area cut out in the centre measuring 195 mm × 180 mm. They were used at the junctions of the main flues.
2   From the Caerleon *Vicus* site comes a rectangular tile measuring 290 mm × 280 mm × 40 mm thick, in the centre of which there is a rectangular cut-out measuring 80 mm × 70 mm.
3   In the Grosvenor Museum at Chester there is a right-angled fragment of tile (probably from Holt) with arms 305 mm × 260 mm and with a width tapering from 60 mm to 50 mm. The inside measurements of the angle are 190 mm × 170 mm. This would seem to be part of a 'frame' as found in items 1 and 2 above.

There is one form of *cuneatus* which because of its unusual shape, sometimes with 'wings', has been referred to by Graham Webster as an 'armchair' voussoir. The purpose of the shape is to accommodate flat tiles, and thereby form a series of open spaces or voids which would lighten the weight of the whole roof. They could also provide ducts for heated air if necessary. A drawing of the roof at Chesters shows the system clearly. (Bertram, 1931, 281 and fig.8)

At Chesters the voussoir was made of tufa, but there are at least twelve sites where those made of clay have been found. Window and relieving arches can be made of flat tiles.

Brick in walls

There is little evidence in Rome of solid walls that are constructed throughout of bricks. It was however common for builders to face walls with broken or triangular brick, and the interior of the walls was packed in with rubble and concrete. The longest edge of the brick was set to face outwards, and is now usually visible, though originally it might have been covered with stucco, plaster, or marble. From outward appearance a wall thus built would seem to have been made of solid brick. A reproduction from the work of Piranesi (Antichita Romane, 1748, Tom. III.V) shows exactly how

20   Walls with facing bricks as recorded by Piranesi

the triangular tile was set into the wall of a tomb structure from the Appian Way.

Several types of brick could be cut up to provide suitable triangles, which can often be detected by observation of the broken or sawn edges. It was possible to saw in half as many as 20 to 30 *bessales* at a time if they were tightly clamped together (Lugli, 1957, 541). These *half-bessales* would produce triangles measuring 305 mm × 215 mm × 215 mm. A *sesquipedalis* brick when cut up could produce eight triangles each measuring 322 mm × 225 mm × 225 mm, but these were more liable to break. A *bipedalis* brick could be cut up to make as many as sixteen triangles each measuring 285 mm × 215 mm × 215 mm.

There is little chance of seeing in Britain many walls that appear to consist solely of brick, though some walls have bonding courses up to as many as six rows deep (e.g. The Jewry Wall at Leicester), and give a first impression of being a mass of red brick. There are however a few impressive examples of solid chunks of brickwork, including those from London (Lombard Street, Bush Lane, and Lower Thames Street), Silchester, Colchester, Lincoln, Ickleton, Ridgewell and Eccles. Hardly any examples of triangular brick have been found in Britain, but it is stated that some examples found in London were in the old Guildhall Museum. (Lethaby, 1923, 15). These are now lost, but some triangular tiles were found in the cheeks of a furnace at Gadebridge Park, and others showed diagonal score lines intended to facilitate the fracture. (Neal, 1974, 14, 15)

A possible reason for the apparently scanty use of brick–faced walls in Britain may be that stone and flint, so readily available, were, with the occasional help of tile courses, quite adequate for the building of walls. Much depended on local natural resources, and in certain parts of this country stone roofs and stone *pilae* are more common than those made of baked clay; indeed in the latter part of the Roman Occupation, tile and brick for some reason seemed everywhere to be used less frequently and to be of poorer quality than before.

The isolated examples of Roman buildings which have survived to something approximating their original height (Appendix ii) remind us of the vast disintegration over the years as a result of natural collapse, weathering, and even more by deliberate demolition, especially where there was quarrying of Roman tile for re-use. We have an occasional glimpse in early writings of what there was once to see. The unknown author of the seventh century elegy known as The Ruin, traditionally supposed to concern Roman Bath sacked by the West Saxons in 577, wrote:

And so these halls are wastes,
The once purple gates and the bricks and wood are lying
Scattered with the smashed roofs. Death crushed that place,
Struck it flat to the hill . . .
(Trans. Edward Morgan)

Even five hundred years later many remains were still high-standing: Giraldus Cambrensis (1145–1214) describes Caerleon in a way that echoes the slightly earlier writings of Geoffrey of Monmouth. In his book 'The Journey through Wales' (1188), he writes:

'You can still see many vestiges of its one-time splendour. There are immense palaces, which with the gilded gables of their roofs, once rivalled the magnificence of ancient Rome. . . There is a lofty tower, and beside it remarkable hot baths, the remains of temples and an amphitheatre. All this is enclosed within impressive walls, parts of which still remain standing. Wherever you look, both within and without the circuit of these walls, you can see constructions dug deep into the earth, conduits for water, underground passages and air vents. Most remarkable of all to my mind are the stoves, which once transmitted heat through narrow pipes inserted in the side walls and which are built with extraordinary skill.'
(Trans. Lewis Thorpe, 1978, Book 1, ch.5)

The sight of such remains must have been most impressive, and they continued to stand for centuries to hold the attention of such later historians as Leland, Camden, Stow and others whose writings and illustrations show what we have lost both in pleasure and information.

Flooring

Apart from a brick pavement at Caulonia dating back to the fifth century BC there was little evidence of early use of brick for floors in Italy (Blake, 1947, 305). Experiments in paving appear to have begun in various parts of Italy towards the end of the second century BC, and the most lasting of these was an arrangement of brick, now known as Herringbone, which Vitruvius refers to as *opus spicatum* or *testacea spicata* (VII, 1, 4), namely brick set as grain in an ear of wheat (*spica*). In his reference to *testacea spicata* Vitruvius uses the epithet *Tiburtina* as though the town of Tibur (Tivoli) was well known for manufacturing these special small bricks. Another town to be associated with bricks was Venafrum, which Cato (234–149 BC) recommends as a suitable place for their purchase (De Agri Cultura CXXXV, I).

Of the laying of these bricks in herringbone fashion. Vitruvius adds: 'They must be carefully handled so that they do not present gaps or ridges, being spread out and rubbed to a level. After the rubbing down, when they are completely smooth and finished, marble dust is sprinkled over, and over that coats of lime and sand are to be applied' (VII, I, 4; Loeb trans.).

There is evidence from Roman Britain of some 30 sites at which

21   Herring-bone floor from Piddington

examples of *opus spicatum* have been found. The individual pieces
vary in size from being 155 mm long (Silchester) to only 70 mm
long (Exeter), and from being 90 mm wide (Holt) to only 30 mm
wide (Great Chesterford); in depth the range is from 60 mm
(Chester) to several examples from elsewhere only 20 mm deep.

This wide range seems to fall roughly into two basic types, one
having the shape of a playing card, and the other closely resembling a
modern 'fish-finger'. But each type has its varieties, and there can be
no standard example of an *opus spicatum* brick. It is possible however
to calculate an 'average sized' brick, which works out at 14.4 mm ×
62.8 mm × 26.3 mm.

According to Winbolt in his report on Wiggonholt (1937, 20 and
21 and fig.6) 20 bricks would have been needed to cover an area of
21 inches × 8½ inches (102 square inches). Evidence is sparse and
for some sites it amounts to no more than a handful of pieces, just
enough to show that *opus spicatum* once existed.

Fortunately however some reports give some definite information:
'The frigidarium of the public baths at Calleva had a central part of
its floor paved in small bricks set herringbone wise' (Boon, 1974,
127). At Verulamium Building IV, 3 was paved with herringbone
and it was suggested that such paving was very suitable for a stable
or cartshed. (Wheeler, 1936, 100) Several herringbone floors have
been found in London (Lethaby, 1923, 27) and at Ashstead one may
have belonged to a kitchen (Lowther, 1927, 151). At Fishbourne a
number of bricks, mostly deep red or blue, were found all in first
period levels – which show no sign of being worn or used, and may
be builder's rejects or surplus from a Period I bath suite at present
largely unexcavated (Cunliffe, 1971, 44–5). One herringbone floor
that can still be seen *in situ* is in a small room near the Old Work at
Wroxeter, and other such floors have been found there (Kenyon,
1940, pl.66c and 71).

Winbolt produced an account of herringbone floor at Wiggonholt:
it concerned a courtyard measuring 19 feet 9 inches (6 m) by 11 feet
(3.35 m) (1937, 21 and fig.6):

> The herringbone floor of the courtyard (Room II) is remarkable –
> probably unique – in its state of preservation. It is 5½ feet below present
> ground-level. There are only three small breaks in it (one of them
> repaired crudely in Roman times), though the SPICAE are laid in lines
> which can hardly be called straight. We describe in detail a length of 1
> foot of a SPICA. The tiles set edgewise are 5in long and ¼in wide, and
> with their mortar joints ten of them go to a foot. The width from point
> to point is 8½in. Thus for an area of 12in by 8½in twenty tiles are

required. The depth of these tiles, when best preserved, is 2½in, but originally they were probably not less than 3in deep. The floor belongs to period I and so was in use all through the life of the villa, some 230 years; this is not surprising with such fine solid work. It must have been worn down considerably by the tread of feet through so many generations, and in places of special wear is now barely 1in. The tiles, as is usually the case, were baked in this small form (cf. those at Ashstead), and were set in a very solid concrete bed, which is 8in deep and laid on a thick base of rubble.

Pieces of brick used in *opus spicatum* are not only irregular in size but also in colour. Collections of brick from Eccles, Fishbourne, and Colchester in particular show a wide range of colour – orange, red, pink, buff, yellow, mauve, blue, and grey; possibly there was some intended polychromatic arrangement, or variegated as in the long corridor at Piddington. In one section the bricks are orange coloured, the next is made up of pinkish-buff brick, while further on there is a patch of bluish brick. The whole stretch is most colourful.

There are several oddities worth noting. One brick from Holt has small roulette marks, one from Leicester has part of what seems to be a signature, and at Wroxeter, among bricks of a herringbone floor was a piece of similar size, but made of a thick chunk of amphora pottery – a most unusual find. (Pers. comm. Graham Webster)

More elaborate varieties of paving used small bricks cut into various shapes. An early example is a brick pavement in pre-Samnite levels at Pompeii (Regio VII, xiv, 5 beneath Casa della Regina d'Inghilterra) (Blake, 1947, 305), where the bricks are scale or lozenge shaped. It was more common, especially in Northern Italy, to use geometric shapes, e.g. triangles, squares, rhomboids or hexagons. Blake believes many such floors to be Augustan, and that moulded rather than cut bricks were used with the purpose of representing more expensive coloured marbles and limestone, i.e. *opus sectile*. The best examples in Britain of geometric flooring come from Silchester in House I, Insula XXIII, and House 2, Insula XXIV. In the former the design of the pavement as originally intended consisted of a border of two rows of tiles, 8½ inches square, the enclosed space having octagonal tiles of the same size with small square ones to fill the interspaces. (Ward, 1911, 260) The two floors seem to have been laid in porches subject to a good deal of hard wear.

From another room at Silchester in the south-east corner of Insula I, polygonal bricks have been removed and relaid in the floor of a summer-house at Wasing House. The bricks here measured 160 mm across (Boon, 1974, 43); this relates to several examples of polygonal bricks stored at Reading Museum, where there are seven hexagonal examples and nineteen octagonal ones.

A pavement of hexagonal blocks was found in the baths at Caersws Fort, Monmouth. To quote Davies (1857, 100): 'The bricks were not more than 3″ superficially, some deep red and others light brown. . .' He points out that since the hexagon form is a honeycomb shape, one mould would serve for all, whereas an octagon would require two separate moulds.

Other hexagonal tiles of grey-buff colour were found in flooring at Fingringhoe, Essex (V.C.H. Essex iii, 1963, 172). Such tile is said to be much more common abroad especially in the Danubian regions, where floors of fancy-shaped brick are frequent. (Boon, 1974, 209). No doubt these floors were meant to represent *opus sectile*, or cut stone flooring, which is rare in Britain, though one can be seen at Fishbourne (Cunliffe, 1971, 33). One would like to know more about the lozenge-shaped tile found at Birdoswald (Bruce, 1863, 26), and also about the odd-sized brick (110 mm × 110 mm × 30 mm) found at Southwick. A floor of check pattern was seen in Room III at Bignor: it was made up of black and red tile in 6 inch squares (150 mm) and resembled a floor seen at Silchester (Lysons, 1817, III, 4).

Far more common than the floors just discussed were floors of plain brick. At Beauport Park, for example, the entrance room is paved with *bessales*, except where the underfloor drain runs, which is covered with *sesquipedales*, which cover exactly the space usually filled with four *bessales*: Room V is paved with inverted *tegulae*, Room IV with *sesquipedales*, Room IX with these and *bipedales*, which became so worn and cracked that they had a surface of cement put on top. At Wroxeter a floor is made of *lydion* (Leighton 1789, 325). At Acton Scott there is a floor of *tegulae* covered with a surface of clay. At Silchester some rooms are paved with *bessales*. At many sites, quarter-round clay covings run round the skirting, sealing the floors with the walls, which made cleaning and sluicing easier.

Brick for Columns

Though clay tiles for roofing in Sicily and southern Italy date back to the sixth century BC, brick was not widely used until the third or second century BC; after the Roman annexation of Sicily as the first province in 241 BC brick was generally used for construction of peristyle columns (Wilson, 1979, 11). At Morgantina for example several houses have columns composed entirely of individual circular bricks which are 380–400 mm in diameter and 80 mm thick (Wilson, *ibid.* pl.2, 1a). An alternative method for columns was to use segments of brick, as at Pompeii.

In Roman Britain wherever circular brick has been found it seems to have been used to make *pilae*, and there is little evidence of it being used to make columns, but other forms of brick have been used for this purpose, and they fall into three types.

1 Semicircular Brick

Of the 28 examples from fifteen sites all but six are complete. Since a great quantity were required even for a single column, the finds seem very few. The complete examples range in diameter from 520 mm at Gelligaer to 230 mm from Wykehurst Farm. The thickness ranges from 80 mm (Caerleon) to 40 mm (Chichester). The diameter does not always exactly equal twice the radius since some are slightly flattened semicircles, but the average diameter comes to 344 mm which once again suggests that the Roman *pes* was being considered.

It seems likely that the bricks were made in a circular mould and then bisected: the cut across the line of the diameter is often more cleanly made than the edge of the circle. Examples only from London and Caerleon carried signatures, and only those from London were stamped.

Several examples have an exact provenance: those from Fishbourne came from the third period plunge bath in the east wing where they were not in fact creating columns, but were used for making seats; others of smaller size from Fishbourne were plentiful in first period levels, presumably for making half or full columns (Cunliffe, 1971, 44).

2 Quadrants

These are like four equal-sized slices of a round cake. Examples from Springhead and Darenth could have formed columns with diameters of 600 mm and 390 mm respectively.

There are two oddities worth mentioning: at Fishbourne among the clay quadrants was one cut from stone, presumably fashioned in order to fill a shortage; at Stebbing quadrants were used to form circular *pilae*, which appears to be a unique use.

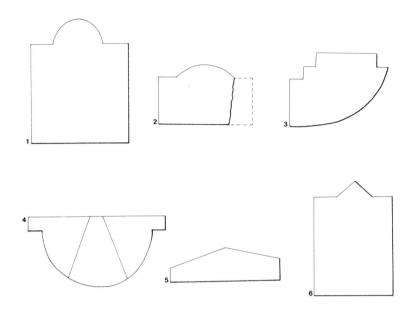

22 Varieties of segmented brick
    1. Park St, St Albans. (Scale ⅛); 2, 3. Verulamium (Scale ⅛); 4. Triple
    brick for half-column. (Scale ¹⁄₁₂); 5. Silchester (Scale ⅛); 6. Castle Dikes
    (Scale ¼)

3 Segmented brick of various shapes

Brick of unusual shape was sometimes used to create semicircular
pilasters of what Lowther (1937, 34) referred to as 'cylindrical
terminal pylons'. Some of the shapes that have been found are
illustrated here.

Sometimes columns were created by more than four pieces. At
Colchester a column had been made up of eight pieces of brick
(Lethaby, 1923, 17), and at Verulamium a column of 2 feet 10 inches
(860 mm) diameter had been created of various miscellaneous pieces
(V.C.H. Herts. iv, 1914, 131).

There is one rare suggestion that semi-circular tile, resembling an
enlarged version of *imbrex*, could have been used to create columns
with two put together to form the circle. In his illustrations of tile
from Bath, Scarth shows some curved tile carrying decoration which
forms a semi-circle with a diameter of 13 inches (230 mm), and he
suggests that this tile was used to make columns (1864, pl.36).

Oblong Brick and other brick oddities

This brick is one of the oddest among the collection. There are sixteen complete examples as well as eleven fragments which seem mostly to be halves of a whole brick. These come from thirteen different sites. The average width of these examples works out at 140 mm and the thickness 47 mm; there are two varieties of length, some are about 240 mm long and others about 440 mm long (similar to the 1 foot 6 inch *sesquipedalis*). One of these longer varieties measures 440 mm × 120 mm × 45 mm and comes from Colchester. A half-example of such a brick was observed *in situ* in the Amphitheatre at Caerleon, and carried a large X signature, which is seldom found.

There is another form of brick similar in size, but pointed at the ends, which comes from the kiln at Holt: it measures 540 mm × 150 mm × 52 mm (Grimes, 1930, 136, 41, pl.3; Nash-Williams, 1969, pl.vi.19). No other similar brick has been found elsewhere:

There are several other bricks whose dimensions do not fall into any standard class. They are all single finds and in the hopes of tracing others a full list is given here.

	long (mm)	wide	deep		long (mm)	wide	deep
Angmering	610	430	65	Wiggonholt	250	180	40
Castlefield	610	400		Canterbury	240	152	12
Holt	580	295	35	York	260	130	35
Heckington	530	290	50	Chichester	240	120	50
Chichester	520	355	25	Crookhorn	185	130	70
Fishbourne	490	310	25	Highdown	205	107	65
Chesters	350	200	45	Silchester	220	110	
Richborough	330	260	30	Slack	290	150	65
London	330	220	70	Brecon	245	180	50
Colchester	290	200	90	Templebrough	150	80	40
Wroxeter	290	190	55				

Other varieties include Cornice bricks of which some complete examples have been found at Caerleon. They measure 405 mm long × 150 mm wide × 75 mm thick : one carried a stamp of Legio II. Caerleon also produced a T-shaped brick (Lee, 1862, pl. xxii, 8), while from Boulogne comes a broken object labelled 'Plinth' which carried an indented Fleet stamp.

One brick from Colchester is very unusual – a rectangular piece measuring 430 mm × 300 mm with the centre scored in squares. Attached to this is a square addition of 80 × 80 mm extending the

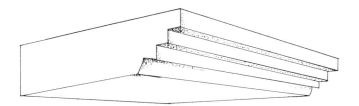

23 Part of cornice brick from Caerleon. (Scale ⅛)

300 mm side to 380 mm, thus making the whole brick roughly L-shaped.

Parietalis (Facing Tile)

Most interior walls of buildings in Roman Britain were plastered over and then painted in various ways ranging from a plain colour, e.g. Pompeian red, to elaborate figured designs. There is, however, evidence that some walls were lined with tiling, though little of this can now be seen *in situ*.

In the Dartford Museum, among the remains from Darenth, is a fragment 80 mm × 60 mm of what is recorded as 'ornamental red tile which formed a kind of dado in two of the rooms'. The thickness is 20 mm. The fragment is decorated by roller impression of compass type. There is also another piece which is slightly larger and comes from Farningham; it has a similar pattern but is not so thick, being only 12 mm. These seem to be the only examples of thin tile being used as a decorative dado.

From eighteen sites there are 30 examples, only five of them complete, of tile that was set vertically to line walls. The chief evidence for this is the nail hole or notch in the side which shows that nails or cramps have been used for attachment. The examples from London, Shakenoak, Mancetter, and Braughing have notches, while those from Richborough, Highdown, Chester, and Cirencester all have nail-holes. The three complete examples, two from London and one from Cirencester, measure 400 mm × 260 mm, almost normal *Lydion* size, but they tend to be slightly thicker.

The other revealing feature of this tile is rough diamond-shaped or lattice scoring on the reverse side. This scoring is similar to that

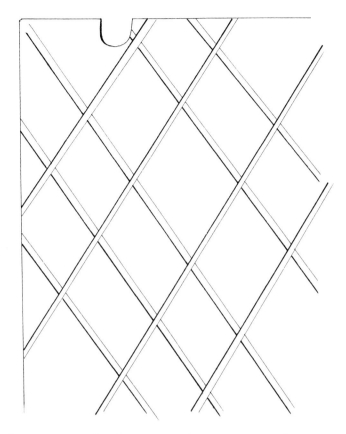

24 Wall-tile from Mancetter showing a cut-out in one corner to take a cramp, and the usual scoring on the face. (Scale *c.* ¼)

found on half-boxes, and the purpose was the same, to aid the adhesion of plaster which was still attached to some examples.

Tile vertically attached to walls would give some opportunity of providing a space through which hot air from the hypocaust could be conducted in the manner of box-tiles, but this space could be created only by fixing spacers looking like bobbins or cotton reels between the wall and the tile (see section of Spacer-Bobbins). At Canterbury, though the wall tiles have been robbed, there are the remains of the long T-shaped cramps (some with bobbins) still fixed to the walls, and these are spaced at points 400 mm × 260 mm apart, as might be expected. It is unfortunate that no site has yet produced bobbins together with wall-tiles, and though this may be the result of robbing, as at Canterbury, it might suggest that there were times when these vertical tiles were attached direct on to a wall without creating any space.

There seems to be no classical term or indeed reference to wall tiles such as this, so they may be given the label *parietalis*, the adjective connected with *paries* meaning a wall. There is a graffito which may support this; it is roller-impressed and occurs on tile from Plaxtol, Kent and it reads: 'Parietalem (tegulam) Cabriabanus fabricavi', '*I, Cabriabanus, fashioned this wall-tile*'. There is a similar, but not identical example from Darenth (Philp, 1971, 297–8). One puzzling point is that the tile on which the graffito occurs is in fact a hollow voussoir tile, not of the wall type discussed here. One explanation for this is that the roller stamp has been used on a tile for which it was not intended, or perhaps the word *parietalis* may have a wide general meaning concerning anything that could be attached to or concern a wall, e.g. a *tubulus cuneatus*.

Tegula Mammata (Type A)

Reference has already been made to brick that carries upon its surface deliberately made lumps of clay in various formations. The earliest find of such brick in Britain would seem to be that reported by the Revd. J. Lyon when excavating St Mary's Church, Dover in 1778. Though he does not refer to these lumps by name there is evidence of them in his drawings (1779, 325 pl.27, and 1813, 366 pl.1).

Since then there has been occasional reference to such brick, and various terms have been used. Those from Alfoldean Bridge were referred as 'nipple tiles' (Winbolt, 1922, 104); tiles found in London in 1887 were later described as having 'rough clay stubs for attachment' (Lethaby, 1923, 25); finds from Highdown included 'brick with knobs' (Wright, 1939, 78); bricks from Holcombe had 'three large projections for keying' (Pollard, 1974, 87 and pl. xxiv c). In reports on tile from Verulamium (Wheeler, 1936, 141) and Fishbourne (Cunliffe, 1971, 43) the word 'boss' is used. These references are given in some detail to show that though such brick was probably found more often than it was reported on, the true nature of it was not freely recognised. Sir Ian Richmond however finally referred to some brick from Bodiam (1966, 99 footnote) as *tegula mammata* (*mamma* = a breast), thus giving it its classical name,

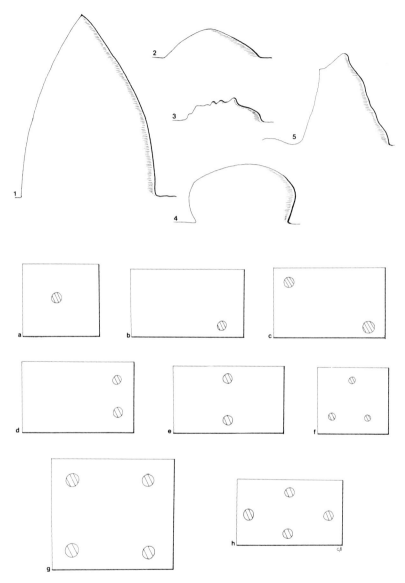

25 Top. 1. Braughing; 2. Bardown; 3. Bodiam; 4. Beauport Park
5. Usk
Bottom.   Different formations and positions of mammae

as originally used by Vitruvius (VII, 4, 2) and Pliny (XXXV, 46, 159).

In the survey, there are more than 50 sites which provide examples of *tegulae mammatae*. They fall into two types: Type A have round shallow *mammae* with an average base diameter of 44 mm and a depth of 17 mm; Type B have conical *mammae* with a base diameter averaging 57 mm and a greater depth of 60 mm. The distinction of the type lies in its purpose. Type B seem to be created for brick set vertically in a wall to create a cavity for insulation or to act as a flue; this type is discussed in the next section. The purpose of the *mammae* of Type A seems to be to assist bonding when the brick was used in courses or for flooring.

The rounded shallow *mammae* are lumps of clay either luted superficially to the surface or bedded into it in a scooped-out hole, as can be seen in section on broken brick. The *mammae* vary in form: some are smooth and bun-shaped like the examples from Beauport Park, Bodiam, and Folkestone; more usually they are shallow and roughly made like rock-cakes. The lozenge-shaped example from Southwick is an odd variation.

There are several different formations of the setting of the *mammae*. Sometimes the *mamma* has become detached, displaying the cavity from which it came, and sometimes the *mamma* seeems to have been chipped off deliberately to make it flush with the surface, e.g. those from Chitcombe and Braughing. *Tegulae mammatae* have seldom been found *in situ* in Roman Britain, but at Beauport Park *sesquipedalis* brick forming the floors of two rooms have the *mammae* facing dowards to make a good fix into the cement beneath.

Full details of sites and provenances are given in Appendix iii. A very high percentage come from South East Britain. *Mammae* do not occur in the known military bath-houses of northern Britain (Gillam, 1978. 389, note 116). There is a strange group from seven sites in which the *mammae* have been superimposed on top of heavy combings.

It has been suggested that the *mammae* were meant to act as spacers when the tiles were stacked in a kiln. This was first proposed by Wheeler (1936, 141), and supported later by Jenkins (1956, 45), and Cunliffe, who wrote that: 'It is reasonable to suppose that the bosses were intended to keep the bricks apart during the firing so that the air could cirulate freely'. (1971a, 43). This seems unlikely, for if the *mamma* was really a necessary part of the stacking process, it would surely be found more commonly than it is, and more tile would carry the marks left after the removal of the *mammae*.

CHAPTER 3

CAVITY WALLING

An obvious development of underfloor heating by hypocaust was to carry heat into space behind the walls round the room. In due course the invention of box-flue tiles proved the most satisfactory means of achieving this. They were easy to handle and attach, and the air was able to move laterally through vents cut out of the side of the boxes. But before such tiles came into general use, other methods were tried for the creation of flues. One early form of flue may have evolved from the idea of creating a cavity wall to avoid damage to wall-paintings through dampness, as expressed by Vitruvius in some detail (VII, 4, 2). He explains how on the top of specially prepared footings flanged tiles could be mounted vertically attached by cramps, they could cover the whole wall and the depth of the flange provided a cavity.

A good example of this can be seen in the vertically mounted *tegulae* in the lower courses of a wall in the Triclinium in the Domus Liviae on the Palatine. Reports suggest that *tegulae* were used in this way in Britain at Woodchester (Lysons, 1797, 13 and pl. xxvii 2.3), at Acton Scott and at Netherby (Acton, 1846, 343).

Tegula Mammata (Type B)

Another way of providing a cavity behind the walls was to mount vertically flat brick which had bosses about 70 mm deep attached near the corners. Such brick, known as *tegula mammata*, was held in place by cramps or T-shaped nails and would allow a more easy flow of air than flanged *tegulae*. Examples of these *in situ* can be seen in an underground room near the Neronian Nymphaeum in the Domus Transitoria, where *tegulae mammatae* were placed to form a series of air shafts, though only the bottom course remains; the tiles measured 600 mm × 600 mm × 40 mm.

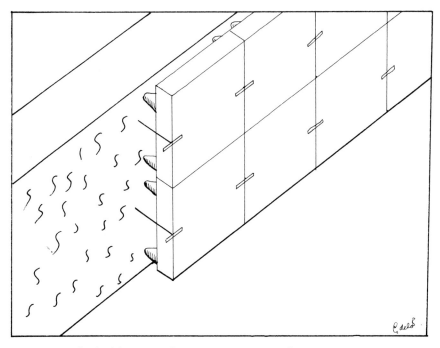

26   One method of fixing tegulae mammatae to a wall

In the Forum baths at Pompeii a whole room is lined with *tegulae* set in the Vitruvian manner. The method is different in the *caldaria* of the Stabian baths where tiles 490 mm square and only 25 mm thick each have four *mammae* 60 mm deep of a conical shape. Mounted on the wall at one end there are a number of *tegulae mammatae* with the tops of the nails holding them still clearly visible. It is suggested that these nails went right through the *mammae*, (Ward-Perkins & Toynbee, 1949, fig.3). A similar method of fixing by the nails right through the *mammae* was found at the House of Pollio at Pausilypon.

Other examples of *tegulae mammatae* still *in situ* can be seen in the house of Julia Felix at *Pompeii* and in the baths at Pausilypon, a Neronian palace near Naples (Gunther, 1913, 224 and fig.152b). All these examples have *mammae* which provided a space of 50 mm. Gunther regarded these projections as 'legs' and referred to the tiles as 'leg-tiles'. Here, attachment to the wall was made by long cramps, and in the example from Villa Julia Felix these nails seem to be held in small cut-outs at the edge of the tile.

There are four sites in Britain which have produced *tegulae* with *mammae* long enough to create a space to provide good heating. They are all conical in shape, as opposed to the shallow round ones found on other sites, and this shape and their length is the reason why a distinction is made between between the two types. Here is a full note on these Romano-British examples:

1 *Cirencester* The four complete examples are all mounted on *Lydion*-sized brick, the only stratified one being reused in a hearth dated to *c.* AD 80.
2 *Dorchester* (Woolaston Road) Excavations in 1978 produced fragments of *tegulae mammatae* from a bath-house area which could date back to AD 74. The conical *mammae* have a 'trough' around the base.
3 *Braughing* Excavations in 1969–73 produced from a bath-house area dated AD 70–140 fragments with *mammae* having a base of 70 mm, and a height averaging about 60 mm. Notches were cut in the edge of the tile so that nails could hold them. The *mammae* were luted on to a smooth surface.
4 *Usk* Two brick fragments were found in a pre-Flavian rubbish pit, probably dating to *c.* AD 55–75. They must be associated with a bath-house. There is suggestion of a 'trough' round the base of the *mammae*, (Manning and Webster, 1978, 381–3, and fig.9).

Half-box Tile

At Sette Bassi in Italy the space is created by the depth of an extended flange, and it was observed that a cut-away gap in the middle of the flange would enable air to move laterally. (Lugli, 1957, 581)

No special term seems to exist for this type of flanged spacing tile, and sometimes the term *tegula mammata* has been used to cover this type as well as the proper *tegula* with *mamma* attached. There is an example of this use with tiles from Exeter (Bidwell, 1979, 33 n.4). The only other Romano-British reference to *tegula mammata* with a flange seems to be in an illustration of a flanged item from Holt labelled as *tegula mammata* (Nash-Williams, 1969, pl.6, 9), and it is clearly the same as that described by Grimes (1930, 135, 5 ii). It seems more logical to make a distinction between the two types, and to call the breasted type *tegula mammata*, and to refer to that with the deep flange and central cut-away as a 'half-box' (as does Graham Webster (1963, fig.11)), on the basis that the 'half-box' is similar to a large box tile cut in half.

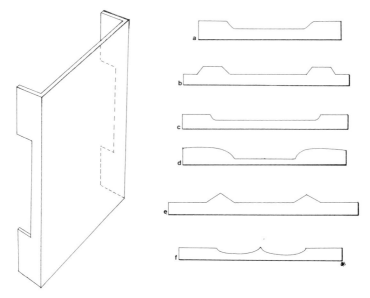

27   Standard type of Half-Box, with varieties of cut-away (Scale *c.* ¼)
     a. Great Witcombe;   b. Chester;   c. Exeter;   d. Hucclecote;   e. Chesters;
     f. Caerwent.

28   Spacer bobbin in situ at Canterbury

Twenty-six sites in Britain have produced examples of these 'half-box' tiles, totalling 42 complete or partial examples. None has been found *in situ*. The average length is 460 mm (about 50 mm longer than the average *tegula*), the width is 330 mm (similar to the *pedalis*) but the external depth of the flange averages 82 mm, which is 33 mm more than the average depth on a *tegula*. This extra depth simply provides more air space in the flue. There are interesting examples from Glan y Mor where *tegulae* which are exactly the same as those used on the roof have been adapted as half-boxes by having the centre section of the flange roughly hacked away.

The cut-away section of the flange usually amounts to about half the whole length, but the shape and size of the cut-away area may vary. The commonest type is angular as seen in examples from London and Llantwit Major, but there are distinctive variations.

Half-box tile usually has large diamond-shaped scoring on the reverse side, but the example from Cirencester has combing. This scoring or combing is an aid to the keying of plaster, and an additional proof that the tiles were set on the wall vertically. One example from London has pink mortar attached which is as thick as 35 mm, made up in two obvious layers. The attachment of these tiles to the wall must have been by large T-shaped cramps or holdfasts.

It is difficult to give precise dates to such tiles, but those from Red House, Corbridge, and the bath-houses at Exeter, Loughor, and Holt could date back to before the end of the first century AD. Similar tiles from Llantwit Major are said to come from the second half of the third century.

Half-boxes are not uncommon on the continent and in an account of tile from the Eighth Legion camp at Saalburg there is a full description of them and the possible method of manufacture of what are referred to as 'hook-tiles' (hakenziegel). (Baatz, 1970, 46 and fig.6).

Spacer Bobbin

Yet another method of creating wall cavity is the use of bobbin-shaped clay objects to form space between the wall and a vertically mounted wall tile. These are held in position by a T-shaped skewer or cramp running through the bobbin. This method was not really considered and investigated until the recent finding of some proven examples, including those from a small second century bath-house at Garden Hill, Sussex in 1972 (Money, 1974, 278–280, fig.2 and pl.57). One was still threaded on its holdfast, but there were no signs of the wall tiles once connected with them.

Since then another example has been found during excavations at Canterbury in 1979 (Tatton-Brown, 1980, 401 and pl.xxiv B). In a small hot room one complete bobbin was found still threaded on its nail, another was almost complete and there were 22 fragments. Since the clamp was intact, the original wall tiles must have been 35 mm thick. Several cramps still in position show the size of the tiles to have been 400 mm × 260 mm – the usual *Lydion* size. They were robbed in Roman times.

A search for other Romano-British examples has produced several that were not originally recognised as spacers. The objects have therefore sometimes been classified among general ceramic oddities. Here are some of the examples, with a brief note on each; those which had no fully penetrating hole must have had some other use.

Wroxeter There are two objects on display in the Rowley Museum, Shrewsbury, and they carry the label: 'Handbricks: not infrequently found on Roman sites. Use uncertain, perhaps for the construction of hollow walls for heated rooms.' One was 80 mm long with a diameter of 85 mm, pierced with a hole of 20 mm.

Binchester A report mentions the finding in the circular hypocaust 'of objects of terra cotta, made exactly after the fashion of a modern

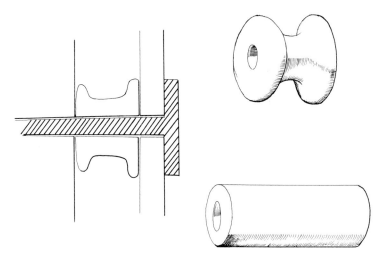

29   Left. A method of fixing bobbin-spacer to the wall

Right. Spacers from   (top) Brockley Hill;   (bottom) Fishbourne. (Scale ½)

bobbin. There were seven or eight or them, none quite perfect, but almost so. They were about 6″ (160 mm) in height, and about 3″ (75 mm) across at the ends. A hole goes through the entire length' (R.E. Hoopell 1891, 21, 63).

Corbridge There is a report of 'Handbricks found in the bath-house, 4″ (100 mm) high, 3½″ (90 mm) across . . . barrel-shaped with a roughly chamfered flange at each end, and each has a cylindrical hole pierced through its axis'. (Forster and Knowles, 1910, 36 and 1911, 50 and fig.39).

Brockley Hill Several Roman items found in Brockley Hill House in 1909 were not reported on until 1955. One object looked like a cotton-reel in red clay measuring 55 cm high, 55 mm across the wide top and base, and 30 mm at its waist. There is a central hole gouged out from each end.

Bothwellhaugh In the bath-house several bobbins about 35 mm high were found, but they have no holes through the middle, nor are there T-shaped clamps in association, and the flue tiles used in the bath-house are of the usual type.

Langton, East Yorkshire The report reads : 'Item 51, black, dirty, with light red outside. An object like a spool or cotton reel. Diameter in the middle about 30 mm.' (Corder and Kirk, 1932, fig. 7).

Other possible bobbins come from Grimston (Laver, 1907, pl. opp 226), Portchester, Elstree, and items labelled 'handbricks' in Devizes Museum. There is a different variety of bobbin spacers in the hollow cylindrical objects found at York, Colchester, Fishbourne (Cunliffe, 1971, 47 item 34), and Chesters (Budge, 1907 items 629–649). They average c. 80 mm in length, with a waist of 55 mm sometimes tapering to 30 mm at each end, and a bore of 20 mm.

Proven examples of bobbin wall-spacers from the continent include those from Themele de la Slaveni (Roumania) where eight items have been regarded as 'Tubuli din hipocaust' for a bath building (Popilian, 1971, 632 and fig.4). One had a central hole pierced by an iron nail.

There is an unusual continental example of cavity walling from the 'Grands Thermes du College de France', Paris in which 'les petits manchons' (muffs) held by iron nails, are positioned in quincunx, one in each corner, and one in the centre (de Pachtere, 1912, 73).

It is odd that on sites where a bobbin object has been found there should be so few examples; since every wall tile would have needed at least four bobbins, there should be a great number lying undisturbed even if the tile was robbed, and there should be more of the cramps that once held them in position.

30   Box-flues at Tindari, Sicily

Tubulus (box-tiles)

Box-tiles are basically a square form of pipe, and have the merit of
being able to stand more securely; they could also easily be mortared
and fixed to the wall to form a continuous battery. Heat could also
have been readily transferred through the thin tile and plaster to the
room. This not only prevented condensation and saved fuel, but also
allowed the baths to operate at a lower temperature, and to have
larger even unglazed windows. According to Seneca (Epistles, 86,

4), the old baths were dark and narrow, but the new ones with their lines of box-tiles creating a continuous *'tubulatio'* were much bigger, and the bathers could enjoy the sunshine and even the view outside. They were able to sunbathe within walls that radiated widespread even heat like that of an electric blanket.

Literary evidence for box-tile is scanty, but Seneca provides some good references: he writes of

> certain devices that have come to light only within our living memory, such as the use of windows which admit a clear light through transparent tiles, and the suspended floors of baths with pipes let into the walls (*impressos parietibus tubos*) for the purpose of diffusing heat, which maintain an even temperature even in their highest as well as their lowest spaces (Epistles, XC, 25).

He refers again (Nat. Quaest. III, 24, 3) to the way in which at Baiae warm air circulated through conduits (*per tubos*), and heated the walls and basins of the baths just as if fire had been applied. Other rooms also could be heated in a similar way. The wealthy could have 'dining rooms that are tempered by hot air passing beneath the floors and circulating round the rooms' (*cenationes subditus et parietibus circumfusus calor temperavit*) (de Providentia, IV, 9).

Seneca, who was put to death at the orders of his old pupil Nero in AD 65, talked of box-tiles being among the inventions of his lifetime. This accords with evidence from Pompeii, where box-flues were being installed with the work incomplete at the time of the eruption of AD 79, and there is earlier evidence from Herculaneum where box-tiles appeared in improvements at the suburban baths made after the earthquake of AD 62.

Heating for baths developed into heating for domestic rooms, and it has recently been shown that passageways and lobbies were also used to conduct indirect heating to neighbouring rooms. (Black, 1985a)

Apart from Seneca's use of the word *tubus* there are few classical references to the equivalent of 'box-tile', but it is clear from some graffiti that the word *tubulus* also could mean a box-tile. The itemised list of tile from Wiggonholt (JRS 30 (1940), 20) includes the entry 'TUBV (LI) N DLX' interpreted as 560 box-tiles; a graffito from Silchester (Eph. Epi. IX 1292 b) reads 'FECIT TVBVL', another from Barnsley Park reads 'TVBL', while one from Dover reads (with restoration) 'TVBULOS DL F' (I made 550 box-tiles), and on a second line, possibly in another hand, is added 'QUASSIAVI LI' (I shattered 51) (Britannia, 4 1973, 332).

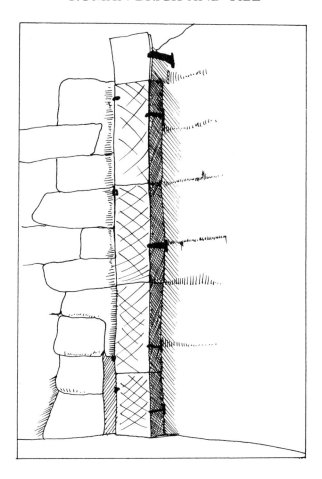

31   Box-flue tiles standing to 1.65m. tall – Beauport Park

The adjective *tubulatus* well describes a room that has *tubuli* in its walls, and Pliny the Younger (Letters, II, 17, 9) refers to a passage-way *suspensus et tubulatus*.

There is some problem in measuring and examining the *tubuli* still *in situ*. Among those sites in Roman Britain where batteries of box-flues can still be seen at floor-level and above are Chedworth, Bath, Binchester, Beauport Park, and Spoonley Wood, while other sites now filled in would include Ashstead (Lowther, 1930, 150 and pl.iii and iv), and Compton (Stephenson, 1915, 44 and pl.ii b).

There is a very rare example of a double row of box-tiles found at Wiggonholt on one side of Room V. As can be seen from an illustration, the boxes are of different sizes, and were set up at different periods (Winbolt and Goodchild, 1937, 24 and fig.8). At Binchester also there is evidence of 'flue tiles two deep at times' (Hoopell, 1891, 15).

It is not often in Britain that box-flues can be seen rising much above the floor level, but at Beauport Park a single flue made up of five boxes still stands intact with its original iron cramps to a height of 5 feet 5 inches (1.65 m) from the floor level.

Box-flues were usually set vertically in the walls, but sometimes they were placed horizontally. Good examples have been found at Great Witcombe – 'On three sides of room 5 funnels were laid horizontally at a height of about 2ft from the floor, communicating with others placed upright' (Lysons, 1821, 181), and at Stroud "In Room 10 box-flues were used to reface the walls arranged in horizontal position along the ground level of the *suspensura* linking with vertical *imbrices* at equal intervals" (Moray Williams, 1909, 40). There is also at least one good example from overseas – the horizontal flues found at the baths at Champvert (Nievre) (Gautier, 1902, 480). Sometimes box-tiles have been laid horizontally beneath the floor, usually to carry heat. Examples have been found at Silchester: "In Room 8 of block ix the whole foundation was made of box flues laid flat to carry heat with a shallow sloping layer of cement laid on top to form a floor" (Price, 1887, 278 and pl.xix). They have also been found at Holt where box-tiles were laid in rows side by side beneath the floor and were connected with the hypocaust (Grimes, 1930, 28). At Bath, however, two small rooms were floored entirely with box-flues laid flat: they butted to the vertical walls and showed no soot (Cunliffe, 1969, 132–3). At Hartlip in Room E box-tiles were used to form a bench or step.

The quantity of box-tiles required depends both on the size of the box and the size of the room. It may be of interest to give some estimated figures. At Beauport Park in Room II most of the hypocaust has collapsed, but in one corner the floor remained intact with lengths of wall measuring 1 m × 0.85 m, preserving a battery of ten box-tiles at floor level. If this section alone had been jacketed to an estimated height of 2.4 m (8 feet) it would have required 73 boxes having a height of 350 mm each. If the whole room measuring only 2.8 m² had been jacketed in a similar way some 190 box-tiles would have been needed.

It is strange that an object that has the single purpose of lining a

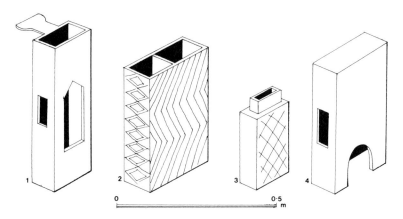

32 1. Box-tile with fish-tail appendage – Ashstead
    2. Double-box – London
    3. Box-tile with socketed end – Gelligaer
    4. Box-tile with cut-out at bottom of the face

wall should have such variations of size and shape. The height ranges
from 470 mm (Angmering – a 'double-box' example) and 450 mm
(Silchester – single-box example) down to 155 mm (Highdown).
The width ranges from 330 mm (Eastbourne – a double-box) and
315 mm (Holt – a single-box) down to 130 mm (Hornby). The
depth ranges from 280 mm (West Mersea) to 85 mm (Colchester)
'Double-box' means that there is a divider down the middle, giving
two partitions. Boxes of this type are rare.

In order to fit properly box-tiles need clean squared-off edges, but
there are examples from eight sites in which the corners are rounded
off both inside and out. This was done deliberately, but there are
other examples where a change of shape may have happened
accidentally. In box-tiles from Darenth, Springhead, and Newport
the bottom has splayed out as though the whole tile has sagged,
unable to maintain its weight because the clay had not hardened.

Some very unusual box-tiles have been found at Ashstead. Instead
of being attached by a T-shaped cramp, a fish-tail shaped appendage
has been fitted at the top of the box and projected as a 3 inch
(70 mm) key into the wall (Lowther, 1927, 1952). The joint of this
projection, even though fitted before firing, must have been very
brittle.

There has often been discussion over the methods of production of box-tile. The theory that a sheet of clay was wrapped round a wooden former raised doubt concerning the possibility of withdrawing the former without damaging the tile, but experiments show that there is no problem in removing the former because the clay stretches, but still remains firm enough to allow the wet tile to stand vertically, and to allow the vents to be cut out in this free-standing position (Morgan, 1979, 395). It is not uncommon to find finger-marks in the area round the vent and deep knife marks can be seen at the angles of the cut. Morgan's examination of sections of the boxes showed that there was only one join, usually on the wide section of the box rather than at the corners.

Sometimes the edge of the face or back has been chamfered, and in a Downton example this sloped trimming has obliterated part of the comb-marking put on previously. A Lympne tile has a chamfered edge and a circular imprint below it.

Style and size of vents

In order to allow the air to circulate laterally cut-out vents have often been made in the sides of box-tiles. Out of 231 complete examples in the survey 83 per cent have some sort of vent. The commonest form is the rectangular vent which averages 77.5 mm tall × 43 mm wide. The largest vent comes on a tile from Wroxeter and measures 150 mm × 75 mm, and the smallest comes from Darenth and measures only 30 × 30 mm. Five sites – Winchester, Chedworth, Rockbourne, Silchester and Ashstead – have box-tiles in which there are two rectangular vents in the same side.

Other vents may be of various shapes; 44 are circular, 11 are diamond-shaped and a few are triangular. Examples with two triangular vents linked together come from Winchester and Guildford, while an example from Bignor is unique in that it has two triangles whose longest side is parallel with the two side edges of the tile.

Certain oddities include one from Bignor which has a circular vent in one side and a rectangular one in the other, a Darenth example has a rectangular vent that is only half-cut out, and one from Newport is unusual in that the sides as well as the faces are combed, with the vent made after the combing.

There is another very rare form of vent which might be better labelled as a 'cut-out', since it is a semi-circular or V-shaped area cut out, not in the sides, but at the bottom of one face. Examples have been found on nine sites. This allowed the heated air to get into the

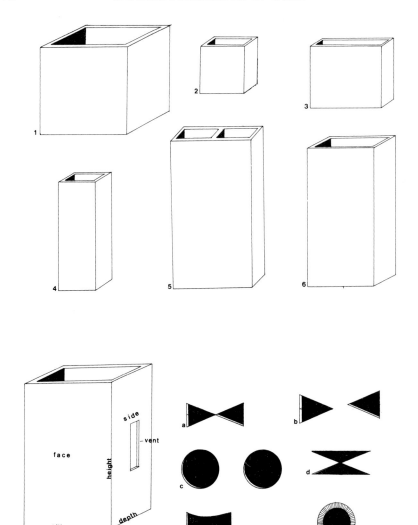

33   Top. Six varieties of shape and size of box-tile (Scale *c.* ⅛)
      1. West Mersea;   2. Holt;   3. Brading;   4. Hornby;   5. Angmering;
      6. Silchester.

    Bottom Left. A drawing to show general features of a box-tile

    Bottom Right. A selection of unusual forms of vent. a. Winchester;   b.
        Ashmolean Museum N.P.;   c. Gelligaer;   d. Bignor;   e. Cirencester;
        f. Binchester

flue system, when flues were built right down to the level of the bottom of the floor of the hypocaust, instead of rising from the floor level above the hypocaust. Sometimes this has not been precut before firing, but roughly chipped out later (Ward, 1911, 276 and fig.84).

Socketed ends

Box-tiles are usually held in place by cramps or other form of nail. There are however a few examples where one end of the box has been shaped so that the end will slot into the open end of the next tile, as in a pipe with a spigot. This form of socketing has been found on boxes from eight sites.

Box-tiles divided into two parts (Double box)

Ten sites have produced an unusual type of box-tile in which the box is partitioned into two sections by means of a central divider. The largest of these examples is taller than any other box of the usual type and comes from Angmering. There is a suggested use of one form of double-box in a report on Ashstead (Lowther, 1930, 146–7 and fig.12). The box has two V-shaped cut-outs at the top and bottom of one of the two sections, and also a circular vent in the face of that same section. The tile seems to have been laid flat resting on tiles above the hypocaust and standing upright on the double-box are box-tiles of the usual type. The two V-shaped vents, now forming a diamond, all come directly underneath the openings of the upright boxes, thus allowing heat from the hypocaust to flow up through them.

The Eastbourne examples carried relief-patterns made by a roller, as also do many other fragmentary examples. Identification of the double-box, apart from the central divider, is assisted by these roller-made markings and the extreme thickness of the walls.

An unusual form of double-box, found at Chester and at Holt, measures 300 mm × 300 mm × 180 cm. Some have circular holes running through each side of one partition: in others the holes come in alternate partitions; since there can be no through draught in these, the purpose is obscure.

Surface treatment (scoring, combing or roller-made relief pattern). One feature which does much to help identify fragments as being parts of a box tile is the evidence of treatment which gave the superimposed plaster a better grip. This is usually on the faces of the tile only.

Of the complete examples of box-tile examined 95 per cent had

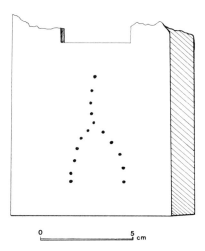

34   Rare Y-shaped punching on side of box-flue

treatment of some kind; of these 33 per cent were scored, 49 per cent were combed and 13 per cent had relief pattern put on with a roller. Scoring means that a sharp instrument or knife has drawn lines across the surface usually in diamond or lattice pattern. Combing means drawing a comb made of wood, clay, bone, or metal across the surface often in quite elaborate patterns. The average amount of teeth on a comb is seven, making an average track of 37 mm.

The only extant 'illustration' of a tile comb comes in an unofficial impression made by a comb on a large brick from Beauport Park (Brodribb, 1973, 333 and pl.xli A). The third kind of marking was put on by means of a roller, which could be used to create quite elaborate, even pictorial, designs.

Though such decorative designs may suggest that they were exposed to view for the eye to enjoy, this is unlikely. Box-tiles were simply butted together, one on top of the other, and if left visible in the walls, smoke and fumes would have come out through the joints. The plaster was put on top of the faces of the boxes for the very purpose of stopping this.

One strange marking is seen on three box-tiles from Beauport Park, and one each from Bodiam, Minety, and Wanborough. It takes the form of a pattern resembling the letter Y punched out in a series of small holes about 2 mm in size. On Beauport Park examples the whole figure is about 70 mm long and 30 mm wide. The marking is always on a sidepiece of box-tile and the single leg points away from the bottom edge of the tile towards the central vent.

Like all other varieties of tile and brick, box-tiles had uses other than their prime purpose as flues. Their use in hypocausts as substitute *pilae* has already been mentioned. They were also used as drains at many sites.

Tubulus Cuneatus (Hollow Voussoir)

Solid voussoirs have already been discussed; hollow voussoirs which may be called *tubulus cuneatus*, have the same purpose, namely to create an arch, but they could also provide airspace either for insulation, or for the flow of heated air. Whereas in the box-tile the open part comes at the top and bottom, in the voussoir it is the sides that are open. The upright tapering parts can be called FACES and there is a TOP and a BOTTOM. In the faces there is often a cut-out vent which enables air to pass from one rib of voussoirs to the next, and most arches would consist of several ribs.

There is a formula by which the span of any arch lined by voussoir tile can be calculated from the measurements of an individual tile. The formula reads: where R = the inner radius of the arch; a = the greater width of the voussoir, i.e. the width at the top; b = the width made less by taper, i.e. the bottom; c = the overall height of the tile, then $R = bc$.

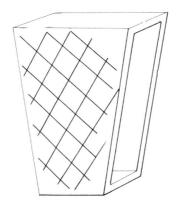

35 Standard type of *tubulus cuneatus* (voussoir) showing tapered faces

At Beauport Park every fragment of tile was kept for investigation, and because the voussoir had obvious characteristics such as a
vent in each face, a small hole in the uncombed top, and a fixed
pattern of combing on the bottom, it was possible to identify and
count the fallen fragments from debris that came from the area near
the long bath. Investigation showed that the pieces represented 212
tops, 213 bottoms, and 420 sides. These closely matching totals gave
evidence of the original minimum quantity of voussoirs. This
deduction may seem theoretical, but the figures are reasonable, and
are mentioned to show the amount of evidence that can be deduced
from very fragmentary material, so long as every piece is carefully
looked at and has enough identifiable characteristics.

The formula when applied to the examples from Beauport Park
gave a span of the arch of 2.55 m (8 feet 4 inches), and it would have
needed some 30 voussoirs to make this arch, always assuming that it
was a perfect semi-circle. The height of the arch above the centre of
the base from which it sprang would have been 1.27 m (4 feet
2 inches); the walls from which the arch might have sprung still
stand at 1.20 m (4 feet), so this gives an indication of the minimum
original height of the room at the highest point of the arch and it may
not have been much higher. The bath was 3.27 m long, so an arch of
2.5 m would have fitted easily on to the ledges at the end of the bath.
The 200 or so voussoirs accounted for would have been enough to
create seven ribs of arching with a depth of 1.47 m. Since the bath
was 1.05 m wide, this arch would have covered the whole bath
comfortably.

There are few instances of any large chunks of arch surviving, but
at Bath where we know that the vault over 'The Great Bath' had a
span of as much as 12 m, there is not only a large section of one of
the lunette ends, but also several chunks of voussoir. One of these
shows six ribs with the open ends visible, bonded on the outside by
broken *tegulae* and *imbrices*. There are no vents in these voussoirs, nor
any sign of soot or smoking, but there are a good deal of drips of
some deposit within the voussoirs. It seems likely that the use of
voussoirs here was simply to lessen the weight of the vault. Many of
the Bath voussoirs had less pronounced taper than those seen at
Beauport Park, which is understandable with vaults of a much
greater diameter.

Another reference to the use of hollow ceramic voussoir comes in
the account of excavations at Silchester in 1906. (Hope, 1907, 442
and fig.3) On at least one example of voussoir from the Silchester tile
collection there is some deposit of what is considered to be calcium

carbonate on the bottom half only of the inside. This has been seen nowhere else except on the voussoirs from Beauport Park where it appears on almost every example, always on the bottom half of the inside and only below the line of the vent. This suggests that hot air within the voussoir condensed and dripped towards the bottom: the presence of this air could have prevented condensation on the intrado of the arch to the benefit of the bathers.

As might be expected with internal roof material subject to inevitable collapse when the building fell into ruin, there are not many complete examples of *tubulus cuneatus* in the survey, and they total only 71 from 28 different sites. There are however a number of partial voussoirs which have the face intact, 110 of these coming from another 42 different sites.

Four sites have produced voussoirs with a type of cut-out that takes the form of a semi-circle on each tapering edge so that when placed next to each other without mortar, a complete circular vent is created. The actual example from Bath illustrated in John Ward's book (1911, 258) was discovered in Colchester Museum. Indeed it was not uncommon to find in Museum collections items from other quite distant sites.

Another form of circular hole has been found in the sides of voussoirs from several sites. This hole is only 25 mm in diameter on the outside tapering down to only 10 mm on the inside. Such a small hole could hardly be used as a linking vent. Equally puzzling are similar tapering holes found not in the sides but on the top of voussoirs from Beauport Park and from Bodiam, a neighbouring site, as well as from Canterbury, Ickham, Reculver, Richborough and West Newton. The examples from Beauport Park and Bodiam differ from the others in that they also have rectangular vents in the

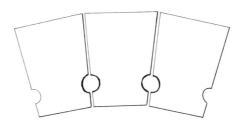

36   Semi-circular cut-outs in the face can provide a link between rows

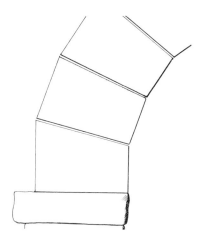

37   The springer acts as a foot-piece from which to mount an arch

38   Hypocaust *pilae* constructed from springers, Canterbury

sides. The purpose of this tapering hole on top of the voussoir is not clear, but it may have been concerned with the handling or setting into position.

The linking-up of the voussoir with the vertical line of box-flues presents a problem, since the opening of the voussoirs are generally bigger and seldom seem to match the opening in the box-flues. Indeed only twelve sites have produced complete examples of both voussoir and box-flue, and those from Newport only made an exact fit. Perhaps the answer is that the voussoirs were set at right-angles to the box-flues with half the opening providing the link for hot-air while the other half rested on a ledge which gave some support for the arch. (Black 1985 b, 355 & fig.1).

Since no voussoir has been found attached to a flue leading to it, it must be assumed that on many occasions the arch was made of voussoirs merely to lighten the weight or provide insulation, and not to carry hot air.

'Springer'

There is an unusual variety of voussoir in which two corners of the face are at right angles, leaving a taper on one edge only. At first sight this seemed to be just a badly-made ordinary voussoir, but the two right-angled corners are clear cut, and any combing pattern follows the unusual shape. This odd variation may possibly be a specially-made tile whose purpose was to act as a foot-piece or springer set at the base of the curved arch, or possibly to change the angle of a line of box tiles. It is not easy to identify a springer from a fragmentary piece, but complete examples have been found at eight sites, namely Clausentum, Chilgrove, Winchester, Minety, Great Weldon, Colchester and Canterbury.

The examples from Canterbury are worth a special mention. There were fifteen of them, and they were all found in the hypocaust of a small room reused to create *pilae* by being set on top of one another.

CHAPTER 4

MISCELLANEOUS

Pipes (*Tubili lingulati*) and Drains

Pipes (*tubuli* or *tubi*) to convey water could be made of hollowed-out wood (Pliny XVI, 81, 224), lead (fistula) or leather (Pliny X, 34, 128), but were usually made of earthenware (*tubi fictiles*); Pliny suggests that the clay *Tubus* was at its most effective for drawing water from a spring when it was two digits thick (1½ inches), and had a socket, rabbet, or tongue (lingua), to link it with its neighbour. In the survey there are 165 items of ceramic pipes or drains, of which 123 are complete examples: these items come from 50 different sites. The pipes are very varied in size and form, the length ranging from 940 mm (Folkestone) to 230 mm (Caerleon), and the external diameter from 23 mm (London) to 57 mm (London).

There must have been many different uses for these pipes, but there is seldom evidence of usage. Some obvious possibilities include internal piping within the bath-house system, the bringing of water into a building and draining it out again, conduits concerned with aqueducts (e.g. near Lincoln), downfall pipes from rainwater, flues and chimneys concerned with wall-heating, and drainage for roadways.

As pipes were frequently below ground-level, it is strange that not more have been found *in situ*, and even those whose find positions have been recorded have not always been in an original position; but at Fishbourne the evidence was more satisfactory, since many pipes 450 mm long (i.e. *sesquipedalis*) were found *in situ* in the garden of the Flavian palace laid to provide water for fountains.

Even when pipes seem intended to be of similar type and size, there is often some variation in measurement. At times, as with some examples from Holt, a pipe in course of production seems to have sagged and grown bulbous, and consequently becomes slightly shorter.

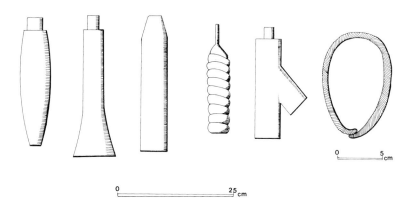

39   Varieties of Pipe. Left to right. Bulbous, flared, chamfered, syringe-shaped,
      jointed, and oval (folded)

These are some unusual shapes:

a.   *Square*

Three large square pipes were found *in situ* at Greetwell in 1925
which are 660 mm long. One end is 230 mm across, and since the
other end is only 190 mm across there is slight taper. Two examples
are combed on alternate sides, and there is the graffito '*Liber esto*' (*Be
free*) on one combed side.
    Another square example comes from Colchester. It is 680 mm
long by 100 mm square, and there is some taper. Another example
from Lincoln appears at first to be rectangular, but is really a round
pipe set in a square concrete jacket, and once formed part of the
Roman aqueduct from Lincoln to Nettleham.

b.   *Hexagonal*

A complete pipe from York is hexagonal with a length of 480 mm,
and a breadth of 100 mm, giving a circular bore of 50 mm.

c.   *Bulbous*

A pipe in Worthing Museum measures 41 cm long and is bulbous, as
are also some Holt examples.

40   Vaulting tubes in situ in hypocaust stoke-hole, Piazza Armerina, Sicily

d.   *Flared end*

An example in the Museum at Cambridge is 510 mm long, and the open end is flared or trumpet shaped. York also provides three pipes 300 mm long which have a slight flare at each end.

e.   *Chamfered end*

An example from Ashstead has no spigot, but one end has been chamfered off to fit into the open end of the next pipe.

f.   *Full length taper*

A Colchester item is 455 mm long. One end with a raised rim is 160 mm in diameter, and the other is 110 mm so the pipe can marry without need of a spigot.

g.   *Oval*

An example from Colchester is 390 mm long and oval in section. Similar oval pipes 410 mm long have been found at Water Newton.

h. *Folded*

Another example from Colchester is 300 mm long, and the pipe has been created by folding a flat section of clay round an oval-shaped former. The section is 100 mm deep, with a perimeter of 230 mm.

i. *Hole in the side*

An example from Colchester is 300 mm long, and 130 mm in diameter. There is no spigot, but there is a hole in the side 75 mm in diameter.

j. *Junction outlet*

A pipe from York is 320 mm long, and has an outlet formed as part of it.

k. *Syringe shaped*

A pipe found in the Castle Grounds at Caerleon measured 235 mm long with a diameter of 75 mm at the wider end. At the other end about a third of the total length tapers off sharply into a nozzle. This gives the whole pipe a syringe-like shape (Lee, 1862, 41 and pl. xxii, 9).

An equivalent of this form can be seen in the Basilica Ursiana at Ravenna, built in 370–396 AD. The half-dome of the great apse is constructed with a spiral of tubes which measure 223 mm long, and one end of the tube forms a thin nozzle that can be inserted at variable positions into the open end of another, and then fixed with mortar (Rivoira, 1925, 259 and fig. 12). At Bath in 1969, though no complete example was found, a number of fragments of ceramic pipes were discovered, somewhat reminiscent of the syringe tube.

A different use of tubular pipes to create vaults can be seen in Room 20 in the Hunting Baths at Lepcis Magna, the pipes being 750 mm long with a maximum diameter of 135 mm. (Ward-Perkins and Toynbee, 1949, 173, and pl. xxxvii e.) Similar vaulting pipes have been found in a bath-house at Morgantina, Sicily, and date back to the third century BC. (Wilson, 1979, 32 and note 64, pl. 2 x). Good examples can still be seen *in situ* at Piazza Armerina, and they are commonly found in North Africa.

This use of piping for vaults may have been derived from the use of *amphorae* or crocks to lighten the weight of a roof. Part or whole pots can be seen in the Stabian baths at Pompeii, in the villa of the Gordiani on the Via Praenestina, and in the tomb of St Helena near

Rome known as 'Tor Pignattara' (from 'pignatta' meaning a pot). Extensive use of pots in this way can be seen in the lower vaulting of the Circus of Maxentius, Rome. (Ward-Perkins, 1981, 424, pl.286)

Few sites in Britain have produced any wide range of pipes, and none equal the collection found at Boulogne.

Though the lengths of pipes are variable there does seem to be some link with the Roman *pes* in lengths of 1, 1½, 2, and 3 feet long (290 mm, 440 mm, 580 mm, 870 mm).

One very unusual pipe to be seen in the British Museum store is 660 mm long with a diameter of 230 mm. At one end there is a small opening neatly cut out of what made a clean flat-cut end, but the other end has a much rougher and wider opening. The exterior is heavily combed. This strange object stands firmly on end, and would make an excellent umbrella stand.

One tile form, clearly a drain, takes the shape of an oblong slab of tile with a semi-circular cut-away all down the centre. It is a type of drain often made in stone, but here made of clay. A rare example in Britain was found in Lower Thames Street, London. There is an illustration, but no size specified (Roach Smith, 1849, 48).

A deeper drain could be formed by making a three-sided object, as also found in Lower Thames Street (Tucker, 1848, 33).

Another use of pipes was to disperse rain-water by down-piping inserted in the wall externally, but few walls in Britain now stand high enough to provide possible evidence of any such practice here, though pipes have been seen set in walls, as for example at Darenth.

At the Forum Baths at Herculaneum similar pipes were inset into the walls to act as a chimney or flue in the early days of the hypocaust heating; and at Red House, Corbridge vertical piping was found *in situ* in the *laconium* which seems to have had the same purpose. (Daniels, 1959, 170).

Hypocaust Material

Though the word *Hypocaust* has become well-known, classical references to it are rare. Vitruvius uses the word *hypocausis* to mean the actual fire, and *hypocauston* to mean the place of the fire (V, 10, 2). Pliny the Younger refers to a *hypocauston perexiguum* attached to a bedroom (Letters II, 17, 23). The most descriptive reference comes from Statius, and it is worth quoting in full:

> Quid nunc strata solo referam tabulata, crepantes
> Auditura pilas, ubi languidus ignis inerrat
> Aedibus, et tenuem volvunt hypocausta vaporem?
> (Silvae, I, 5, 57–59)

which means

> Why need I now mention the paved floor laid flat upon the soil, destined to hear the thud of balls, where the restful warmth meanders through the building and the hot rooms exhale the insubstantial steam ?
> (trans. J. Burgess)

The term *diaetae hypocaustae* is used by Ulpian (Digest, 32, 55, 3).

Among his endless snippets of information Pliny tells us that the hypocaust underfloor system of heating was invented in the early days of the first century BC by C. Sergius Orata 'qui primus pensiles invenerit balineas' (IX, 76, 168). The name 'Orata' may have been a nickname derived from a fondness for golden trout (*auratae*). Orata developed a successful business concerned with oyster beds, and according to Valerius Maximus (IX, 1, 1) he may have originally used his invention for the heating of stone fish tanks.

Vitruvius gives specific instructions for the building of a hypocaust. An early example is found in the Stabian baths at Pompeii. These were originally built in the early years of the second century BC and were later enlarged, though still without hypocausts. When the Forum baths were erected in *c*. 80 BC the *caldarium* was equipped with a hypocaust, and the Stabian baths were then renovated to contain hypocaust heating. The *pilae* or piers however were not made of *bessales*, but of large roof tiles cut to measure 650 mm × 480 mm (Blake, 1947, 307, n.76). (The use of *tegulae* to form *pilae* is very rare in Britain, but in a hypocaust at Beddington some of the outer *pilae* are built up of fragmented *tegulae* laid flat.)

Vitruvius' instructions for the building of hypocausts are as follows: the ground was to be paved with *tegulae sesquipedales* (bricks 1 foot 6 inches square) and made to slope towards the mouth of the furnace (*praefurnium*) to such a degree that when a ball is thrown on the floor it will roll gently towards it. This slight slope is also meant to help draw the flame. Upon this *pavimentum* the *pilae* were built at intervals suitable to take the *tegulas bipedales* (bricks 2 feet square)

41 Diagram to show the setting of *bipedales* with corners resting over capping
on the centres of each pila.

which formed the suspended floor. The function and position of
these *bipedales* causes them sometimes to be called 'bridging tiles',
since each corner of the *bipedalis* has to be sited on the centre point of
four *bessales*; this usually means a gap of about 16 inches (410 mm)
between each *pilae*. He also states that the *pilae* are to stand two feet
high: 'altitudinem autem pilae habeant pedes duo'. The actual
number of *bessales* required would depend upon the thickness of the
bessalis used, which can vary from 25 mm to 7 mm, and the
thickness of the mortar between each tile also matters. The average
number of *bessalis* in a *pila* of two feet would be ten.

42   A general view of the baths block of Chedworth, showing hypocaust *pilae* and box-flues.

Vitruvius does not mention what seems to be a common practice in Britain – the use of a brick one foot square (*pedalis*) as a cap to surmount each *pila*; this not only gives extra support, but helps to fill in any gaps caused by any irregular size of the *bipedalis*. The distance between each *pila* depends much on the size of the capping stones. At Wall where a great number of *pilae* can be seen (or at least the bases of them), the distance from centre to centre of each *pila* seems to be 800 mm; at Beauport Park in Room I the average distance works out at 920 mm. It is clear from any study of hypocausts that the structure is subject to much variation.

It was essential that *bipedales* should lie flat and fit well as otherwise the cement laid on top would run through the joints and lead to the cracking of the overlying surface which consisted either of cement with a smooth finish or perhaps had a mosaic laid on top of that. If the whole foundation had (as Vitruvius suggests) to be set on a slope to help the fire and also to assist draining, the creation of a hypocaust had to be a work of precision. However, evidence of some extant examples of *pilae* shows them to be very rough and ready both in material and structure. Vitruvius talks of *pilae* two feet high, but he gives no figures for the whole depth of the floor from the foundation level to the top surfaces of the *suspensura*. The thickness of this flooring could be considerable and the various levels create a quite complicated structure: *pilae* base, *pilae*, capping tile, large bridging tile, cement (sometimes as much as 300 mm deep), and final top surface.

It would be interesting to know if there is any correlation between the height of the *pilae* and the depth of brick and cement which created the floor above them and whether the size of the room influences their height. In comparing the size of a room with the depth of the *pilae* it must be remembered that the floor of a large living-room would require less heat than that needed in a smaller bath-room, so many fine mosaic floors do not necessarily have deep *pilae*, if indeed they are heated at all. The exceptionally large floor of the Inner Court at Woodchester is 48 feet 10 inches square and is mounted not on *pilae* but on cross-channelled heating flues which are 4 feet (1.22 m) deep. It is not uncommon to heat floors in this way where no extreme heat is needed.

Wroxeter gives good evidence of the variable depth of *pilae* in hypocausts. In a heated room in a house, the depth may range from two to three feet, and a small bath-house from three to four feet, but in the public bath-house they rose to as much as 6–7 feet (Webster, 1960, 8).

In the bath-house at Side on the south coast of Turkey the *pilae* under the central court must be 7 feet tall (2.1 m). In contrast the *pilae* in one of the baths in the great bath complex of Caracalla were only 2 feet 9 inches tall, made up of 13 *bessales*. (Middleton, 1892, ii pl.2) High-standing *pilae* have been found at many sites in Roman Britain. Those in the bath-house at Gelligaer were seldom less than 2 feet 9 inches and sometimes nearer 4 feet (Ward, 1909, 44); at Binchester the hypocaust of the Commandant's bath-house was made up of 17 *bessales*, giving a *pilae* height of 3 feet 6 inches, and the total depth from foundation level to floor surface was some 4 feet 6 inches. At Newport (I.O.W) there is an interesting variation of the *pilae* in the *sudatorium* standing 38 inches high, while those in the *tepidarium* were only 27 inches high (Stone, 1929, 143).

One reason for the comparative shortage of intact *suspensurae* in

43   Hypocaust *Pilae* formed of 2 *imbrices* joined together and filled with mortar, Rockbourne

bath-houses in Roman Britain is that hypocausts tended to collapse when the roof crashed down on a structure whose bricks were already weakened by the intense heat to which they had long been subjected. We know that in the *sudatoria* the surface of the floor above the *pilae*, once it was heated up, could retain its heat to a high degree (Boon, 1974, 125–6). Pliny the Younger tells the story of how some rebellious slaves left their master, Larcius Macedo, to die as he lay on the floor of the hot room in the baths (Epistles, III, 14). Spartianus tells of the great bath building created by Caracalla, which included a 'slipper room' (*cella soliaris*), suggesting a floor of considerable heat (Script. Hist. Aug. Caracalla. IX, 4).

Though *pilae* made of brick provided the most efficient form of hypocaust and coped best with the great heat, sometimes a shortage of *bessales* meant that other types of brick were used either to fill in odd spaces in need of repair or for more extensive use. Alternative forms of making *pilae* include :

1. *Box-tiles*

Usually filled with mortar, these have been found on at least fifteen sites, sometimes throughout the room, sometimes as occasional fill-ins or repairs (e.g. Payne, 1897, 54 and pl. B).

2. *Voussoirs*

Used to form *pilae* on at least two sites, Stroud, West Sussex, and Canterbury.

3. *Imbrices*

At Rockbourne (Room xxix) there is a rare example of every *pilae* being formed of 2 *imbrices* being joined together and filled with mortar to make a shallow hypocaust. (Morley Hewitt, 1968, 22, and pl.3b)

4. *Cylinders*

These are like pipes, but one end has been filled in. They could be purpose made, but none have been found *in situ* in use as a *pila*. In the example from Wroxeter, the upper part has an external diameter of 110 mm, while the base – 90 mm thick and filled in – has an increased diameter of 230 mm. The length is at least 260 mm. There are four deep finger-marks on the underside at the edge of the base. Similar fragments with the same features have been found at Chester and Holt, and there are other possibles from Cirencester and Abingdon.

There is proof from overseas that such cylindrical objects were used to form a *pila* in the site of St Bertrand de Comminges, in the foothills of the Pyrenees. They are about 1 m long with a hole down the centre (Wilson, pers. comm.). Other examples come from Italy at the Via Nomentana bath at Ciciliana, near Tivoli, at a floor at Roma Vecchia, and in the baths at the villa of Voconius Pollio. The villa just beyond the eighth milestone of the Via Praestina known as 'Muraccio dell' Vemo' had *pilae* made of socketed pipes instead of plain cylinders (Blake and Bishop, 1973, 114).

An even rarer means of providing support for underfloor spacing is found in a building just outside the Aurelianic Wall between the Via Appia Nuova and the Via Latina; here the floor rests upon the apexes of triangles made of *bipedales* set *a cappuccio* with the inside of the triangle filled with mortar. The empty triangles in between

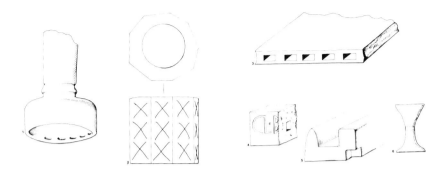

44 A selection of unusual ceramic objects (Scale *c.* ⅛)
   1. Footed cylinder, possibly to act as a pila – Wroxeter;   2. Multi-sided
   object – Kingscote etc.;   3. Slab with slots – Castor;   4. Part of a stamped
   plinth – Boulogne;   5. Possibly a specially made tile to form a gutter – Holt;
   6. Pillar-shaped object – Hunsbury Hill.

created an air space, not for heating, but simply for insulation (Blake
and Bishop, ibid.).

Sometimes the shortage of clay tile led to *pilae* being constructed
of other material such as stone, or even, as at Darenth, of chalk
blocks. In certain areas of Britain, such as the West country, where
stone is plentiful, many buildings were roofed with shaped stone slabs
instead of *tegulae* (Williams, 1971, 95–119), and likewise stone *pilae*
were not uncommon, e.g. at Kingscote where an intact floor is
mounted throughout on stone *pilae*. On several sites a mixture of
material can be seen: e.g. at Great Witcombe, with *bessales* mixed
with monolithic stone capitals and bases, Wroxeter has one
hypocaust using *pilae* of granite or red freestone alongside tiled *pilae*
sometimes mounted on lumps of stone; at Wall there are several *pilae*
made of stone which has not worn as well as the other surrounding
pilae made of clay.

Unclassified or Unidentified Objects

In the course of research several unusual clay objects were discovered. Among these was a group of objects with eight or nine
sides, a diameter of 140 mm and a height of 120 mm. The sides were

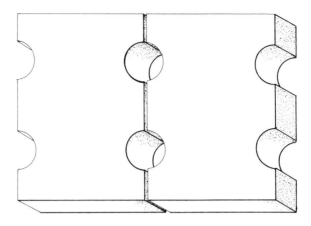

45   Floor tiles from the kiln at Holt showing cut-outs to create vents for heating
to circulate. (Scale ⅛)

diamond-scored. These have been found at Frocester, Kingscote,
Uley, Cirencester and Wanborough – all sites not far from each
other. (Swain, 1979, 9, fig.3).

Objects of a pillared or block shape include those from Peterborough, Piddington, Leicester, Letchworth, Lincoln, Fishbourne,
Alcester and York.

Roughly cut-out circular flat discs with a diameter of about 90 mm
have been found at London, Glan y Mor, Wanborough, Dicket
Mead and Stonea. They may be pot-lids or possibly counters for a
game.

There is a curious slab with holes running through from Castor,
and an oddity from Holt which might have been fixed onto the edge
of a roof to form a gutter. In all, some 50 peculiar objects were
discovered, and it is hoped that further parallels may be found which
will help to throw light on their purpose.

Apart from these there are about 25 objects which were labelled in
catalogues as being connected with kilns. Kilns have been fully listed
and discussed by Alan McWhirr (1979, 97–194), and also in a recent
study by Vivien Swan (1984).

Some of the items are bricks of *bipedalis* size which have semi-
circular cut-outs on the edge. These create vents when the bricks are
laid side by side, and another version for the same purpose is found
in bricks of the same size which have a number of small, tapering
holes. The ones from Chester have been reported in full (Williams,

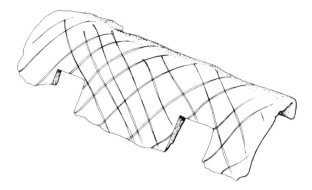

46   Curved scored tile with cut-outs from a kiln at Canterbury. (Scale *c.* ¼)

1895, 79). At Holt oblong brick 400 mm long with V-shaped ends
has been found, presumably of kiln use.

Among smaller objects there are pillar-shaped ones which may be
props or stands, or rough ring-shaped pads like a large doughnut
which are said to be for supporting *mortaria* in the kiln (Grimes, 1930,
183), or 400 mm long objects rounded off like a French loaf with a
similar flat base, found at Ecton and Duston. From Savernake Forest
come circular plates 190 mm in diameter and only 14 mm thick.

In Lincoln Museum there is a one-third size model of the kiln at
Torksey, and this shows several other unusual brick objects. Though
we know something about kiln sites, we really know very little
about the many odd items sometimes known as kiln 'furniture'.

There is an interesting oddity which at first sight appeared to be a
perfect example of ridge tile. This is a complete tile found with
similar fragments at a kiln site at St Stephen's Road, Canterbury.
(Jenkins, 1956, 44–5, fig.3). It is 400 mm long, has very slight taper
from 180 mm to 190 mm and stands 100 mm high. The chief feature
was two sets of rectangular cut-outs on each side as though to fit
over the ends of two adjacent flanges of a *tegula*. The external surface
was scored all over with a lattice pattern in a manner unique for any
form of *imbrex*. It seemed that this tile might be a rare descendant of
the ridge tile with cut-outs mentioned by Blake. But something was
wrong, the 150 mm gap between the two cut-outs was far too
narrow to take the flanges of a *tegula* whose average width is 300 mm
and the cut-outs themselves, though deep enough, were just too

narrow to fit over two adjacent flanges. Another problem was that if the cut-outs were to be made in a series of ridge tiles each 400 mm long in order to fit over adjacent flanges each with a gap of 250 mm between them, these cut-outs would come in different positions on each tile. They could not be precut before firing as in the examples we have, and each tile would have to have a cut-out in a different position. This tile probably had some special use in a kiln.

CHAPTER 5

MARKINGS

Signatures

Very little attention has ever been paid to the markings, often semi-circular, to be found on the face of many *tegulae* and also on bricks. These usually appear without comment in the illustrations of some early writers, e.g. Lysons (1797) and Artis (1828), but one early observation comes from 'J.J. jun' in Isca (Lee, 1862, 41). It reads:

> Wherever the roof-tiles are found, it is singular that they almost universally have towards one end an obscure semi-circular marking, the use of which it is difficult to decide.

Another early reference was that by Williams (1895, 78) who regarded a finger-made mark on a tile from Chester as 'the *signum* of the maker with which he signed his work'.

In later years it was stated that the 'concentric groovings' found especially on the faces of *tegulae* were put on for decorative effect. (Ward, 1911, 263) In discussing tile from Vindonissa Jahn had previously considered the matter more deeply, and regarded the marks as 'limited to basic forms which represented the practice of a guild', and acted as some type of traditional craft-mark, denoting procedure at the kiln; he did not consider them to depend upon the whim of an individual (1909, 121).

Since however the marks were made by an individual, it seems reasonable to regard them as worthy of the name 'signature', hence the heading of this section. Signatures appear more frequently on *tegulae* than any other type of tile.

Signatures on Tegulae

Sixty-five per cent of these take the form of even and symmetrical semi-circles, as if they had been made with the help of a compass, though in fact they are usually made with the tips of fingers. These

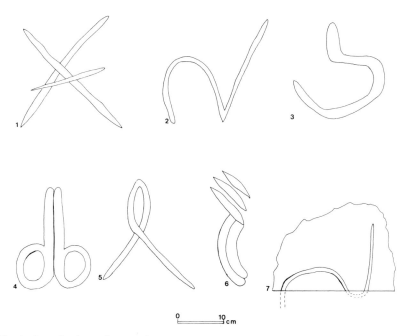

47   1–6 a selection of unusual types of signature;
      No. 7 shows how part of a signature has been trimmed off from the bottom
      of a tegula – Beauport Park.

grooved signatures have been classified according to the quantity of
'half-rings' which range from one to four, and there is one example
from Horncastle which has five. No distinction has been made
between the sizes of the semi-circle either in height or width of base,
or in the amount of spacing between the rings. There are some
instances of a fine line within the groove caused probably by a torn
finger-nail as seen in examples from Ribchester and Beauport Park.

Constant practice would make the quick sweep of the finger or
fingers an accurate form of marking. There are seldom examples of a
finger slipping, or of the rings overlapping (exceptions come on tile
from Wanborough, Silchester and Beauport Park). Personal experiment has shown that a mark with the finger can be put on when the
clay is still quite soft, whereas the die for a stamp can be imposed
satisfactorily only when the clay has become leather-hard.

Of the 41 complete *tegulae* from Beauport Park all but two carry
signatures, but this high proportion may not have been maintained
throughout Britain. Of all the complete examples of *tegulae* in the

Survey 60 per cent carry signatures and two-thirds of these were of the semi-circular variety.

A survey of tile from a particular site gives evidence of the variety of signature. Silchester, which has produced 61 complete *tegulae*, provides nine types of signature. Beauport Park has produced eight varieties. Throughout Roman Britain there is a wide range of signatures, as shown in a selection of some of those that are not of the semi-circular type.

There are several *tegulae* in which the lower part of the signature has been cut off as a result of some trimming on the bottom edge of the face. Examples include these from Wroxeter, Chester, Beauport Park, and Lapworth. It is hard to see why such trimming should have been necessary but the evidence is clear enough, and shows an order of procedure in which the signature was always put on before any trimming. Other evidence of procedure comes from the frequent occasions in which a stamp or an animal impression is superimposed over the signature, e.g. one from Caerleon where a legionary stamp comes on top of the signature, and a tile from Caistor by Norwich which has a paw impression on top of the signature. Wherever stamp and boot/paw marks coincide, the boot/paw mark is always superimposed over the stamp, as is seen in an example from York which has boot mark over stamp, and one from Holt where a dog paw mark has been placed over the stamp.

Signatures on imbrices

There is difficulty with comparison between the signatures found on *tegulae* and those found on *imbrices*, because the *imbrex* does not provide the same wide area of flat surface that can so readily receive marking or writing. For this reason any signature found on an *imbrex* tends to be placed on the side of one corner of the wider end, or across the top of the 'gable'. Little reference has ever been made to signatures on *imbrices*, but in his report on tile from Park Street, St Albans, Lowther noticed a squiggle mark on the corner of an *imbrex* and regarded it as 'ornamental pattern' (Lowther, 1945, 99).

Once again the Beauport Park collection provides useful evidence. Of the 56 complete *imbrices* found there all but one bear either a Fleet stamp (49 examples) or a signature (six examples). The distinction between the two is not clear, and there is one puzzling example where a stamp has apparently been cancelled by a superimposed signature.

Of the 320 complete examples in the full survey, only 41 (14.7 per cent) carry some sort of signature and/or decoration. Sometimes the marker has used a comb instead of his finger. Combing or scoring has usually the purpose of assisting the rendering of plaster or mortar, but combing on the top surface of the wide end of an *imbrex* could have no such use. There is however one fragment from Northchurch which has combing across the narrow end 'to make mortar adhere between two overlapping *imbrices*' (Neal, 1976, 27). It was observed that a modern *imbrex* on a roof at Arles had fine cross scoring across the narrow end for a similar purpose. If the Romans had found such treatment necessary on *imbrices* they would no doubt have used it, and it rather suggests that *imbrices* were often laid on top of each other without mortar.

Among all *imbrices* both complete and partial there are ten different types of markings ranging from simple finger-made signatures to ribbing along the whole length of the crest, as well as eleven examples of combing and one of scoring. Even if some of these resemble decoration rather than signature, they are still marks imposed by an individual.

Signatures on Brick

Out of the 1169 examples of brick only 194 (16 per cent) carry signatures. The table shows the composition of this figure:

Type	Total	Signatures	%
Bessalis	608	54	8
Pedalis	200	33	16
Lydion	297	81	27
Sesquipedalis	42	18	42
Bipedalis	22	8	36
	1169	194	16%

Of the 194 signatures 84 (43 per cent) were of the semi-circular type.

The varying quantities of examples of brick types make comparison difficult, but the *bessalis* (only 8 per cent signed), being the easiest to make, may have been regarded as unworthy of a signature. At Beauport Park, for example, only one of the 79 complete examples carries a signature: on the other hand, at Bignor all but one of thirteen examples carry signatures ranging over eight different types. With larger brick such as *sesquipedalis* and *bipedalis*, which required more skill in handling, there is a higher proportion of signatures, which occur on 26 of the 64 examples (40 per cent) and some of them are most elaborate.

The details given so far have been based on evidence from complete examples, but a great many incomplete examples of all kinds have also been noted, and for a full picture of the range and variety of signatures these partial examples must also be considered. The total of different varieties comes to over 150. It is scarcely credible that so many different forms can be devised, especially when such obvious ones such as the cross and the circle are seldom found. On Saxon pottery a great variety of marks usually made with a die have been found, and an effort has been made to give a meaning to these, e.g. the snake motif is said to represent evil (Myers, 1969, 138–140). Such significance can hardly be applied to the signatures on Roman tile and bricks.

It would be satisfactory to find conclusive evidence that different tile makers (*tegularii*) were concerned with different types of brick. The Beauport Park collection shows that certain signatures are confined to *tegulae* and others to brick of various kinds, but the evidence elsewhere is too scanty to form any firm conclusion.

Of all the different types of signature recorded only twenty-one were put on with a comb, and hardly any scored with a knife or stick; the rest are put on with the finger, and some of these examples are unusual. On one from Box the signature takes the form of five parallel finger-made grooves about 30 mm long, and from Cirencester comes a similar signature made by three deep grooves. Twelve finger types are multiple i.e. made up of two different separately spaced signatures. One Silchester example has the whole surface pitted with jab marks made by a finger tip and an *imbrex* from Newport has in the area of the apex a single, double, or triple finger-tip mark in which the scratch of the finger-nail can be clearly seen.

Because of their individual patterns all examples marked with scoring and combing have been noted on all types of tile. The scoring on the half-box and wall-facing tile is undoubtedly put there to assist the attachment of plaster, but the rare combed signatures on *tegulae* may simply be signatures put on by a man who had borrowed his fellow's comb. Where there is extensive combing on brick this also suggests some keying purpose.

The quantity and variety of signatures raises several questions. The first is why some tile is signed and some not signed. Since brick-making in Roman Britain covers several hundred years, and may be very localised, it would indeed be surprising if there was any universal practice throughout the whole country over the whole period. Each tilery would no doubt tend to have its own customs. That the *signum* has some real purpose is shown by the fact that all the complete brick and roofing tile listed no less than 28 per cent carry signatures, though the percentage is not evenly spread over all types. Comparative figures for tile overseas would be most interesting. Only one is readily available: in a brief survey of tile in the Bas Dauphiné area of France only 20 per cent of the *tegulae* carried signatures, all of the concentric groove type (Chauffin, 1956, 83). The proportion for signed Romano-British *tegulae* was 60 per cent.

The second question raised is what the *signum* represents. One suggestion is that those on *tegulae* are placed near the bottom of the face to act as a guide as to which way the tile must go, and to support this idea is the fact that there is only one example of the signature at the top of the face. But, since the form of the cut-aways at the bottom of the flange clearly indicates which way the *tegulae* must be set, such a mark would surely not be necessary.

If it is to be identified as an individual mark, with each maker having his own, there would surely have to be a great many more to cover all the *tegularii* who operated over the years of occupation.

Another possibility is that the *signum* represents the work of a group in a particular tilery, or even that of the whole tilery, though the many variations of signature found on any one site might argue against this. At Fishbourne a note attached to tiles in a small plunge bath in room 28 states: 'The tiles are incised with concentric rings. These may have been the trade-mark of the factory that made them'. Only the study of signatures from individual tileries can throw more light on the matter.

The use of a trade-mark dates well back before Roman times. The Hindus regularly used marks in their trading with Asia before 1300–1200 BC. Excavations at Nineveh produced brick bearing makers' names (Diamond, 1975, 269). The Romans in their common practice of marking objects, e.g. samian ware, amphorae, oculists' stamps, and brick were following others, and as usual doing it more thoroughly.

It is obvious that Roman tile and brick varies much in quality, and it is interesting to not that a number of very poorly finished *tegulae* from the Beauport Park collection all carry the same distinctive signature, identifying the maker and not very favourably. The 'price-list' issued by Diocletian records a pair of *tegula* and *imbrex* 'of the first quality', which perhaps suggests that different grades were on sale.

More evidence is needed if any conclusions are to be reached, and it is important that all fresh finds of tile should be closely observed to see what range of marking there is, how often the same signatures occur, and whether it comes on different types of brick. This survey has already brought evidence of a link-up of marks on material used on neighbouring sites (e.g. Beauport Park and Bodiam, Bignor and Chichester, Springhead and Darenth), but all such research is still in its very early stages, and it may be some time before the 'message' written in the signature can be clearly understood.

Combing and Scoring

Box-tile and Voussoir

Unlike the signatures or decoration, the indented grooving on box-tile and hollow voussoir tile has the prime purpose of providing a key for the plaster and rendering that covered the tiles when they had been set into the walls or arches. 253 complete examples of tile have been listed, 195 of box tile, 6 of double-box, and 52 of voussoir; 94 per cent of all these were scored or combed or roller-printed, and only 6 per cent left plain. There were also nine unusual examples smeared or dabbed with the finger-tips. A detailed break-down of these figures is given in appendix iv.

Combing

Even though it meant the use of a specially-made instrument, it was more efficient to use a comb than to score the tile with a knife of stick. There is a unique impression of a tile-comb on a large tile from Beauport Park: alongside an official CL BR stamp some tiler has imposed his tile-comb on the soft surface, leaving a clear impression of it. The length from the tip of the handle to the row of teeth is 132 mm, and the row of eight teeth gives a close-set track of 35 mm. Wood grain is evident, and engraved on the surface of the comb are the letters CL BR, though since the comb was never intended to be used as a stamp, they appear retrograde. It is an interesting side-light on tile production that even a tile-comb should carry the official mark. (Brodribb, 1973, 333 and pl. xli a)

Combs made of wood are not likely to have survived, but other materials might have been used. A fragment of box-tile from Griff Hill is said to have had markings imposed by a comb made of bone. (Scott, 1971, 17), and there could be some analogy from a comb

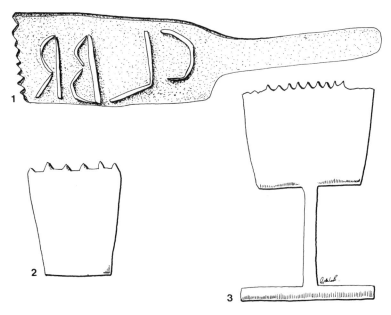

48   Impression of a tile-comb – Beauport Park; (Scale ⅔)
?   Metal tile comb – Witham ½;
Metal tile-comb – from Germany (after Blumlein). (Scale *c.* ¾)

49   A box tile from Holt displays the use of twisting the comb (Scale ½)

made from a cattle-bone used to give rilling round the bodies of Iron-age pottery from Manching, Germany (Green, 1979, 364). From Witham a metal comb has been found that may have been concerned with the marking of tile, though possibly it was used for carding wool (Pers. comm. Robin Turner). The Witham example has no handle, unlike one recorded from Germany. (Blumlein, 1926, 47, fig.137 b)

Though there are few surviving examples of a comb, there are many examples of combing in which the number of teeth on the comb and the width of the resulting track have been carefully noted. The quantity of teeth ranges from 24 to three, and the track width from 105 mm to 18 mm. Some examples had grooves almost too fine to count, and it is not easy to count the teeth from a rubbing, especially when a tooth has been split in such a way that it gives a misleading extra groove, though such flaws are useful for identification.

There are some very elaborate examples of marking with a comb. An item from Leicester has 'Primus Fecit X' written with a comb across the face of a box tile, while from Holt there is a large combed figure like an Arabic number 2. By twisting the comb it is possible to give taper to a track. Such examples required clever handling, and show the enterprise of an individual determined to give identity to his work.

Since the sweep of the comb usually takes it over the edge of the face of the tile, it is rare to see the V-shaped end of the tooth grooves, but such evidence is clear on examples from Carisbrooke, West Mersea, Holt and Heckington.

There are a few examples of what might be called hybrid marking. An example from West Mersea comes from a square box-tile which has scoring on one face and combing on the other; one from Colchester has the same treatment and probably comes from the same source. A box-tile from Leicester has one face slightly combed, while the other three sides have lattice scoring.

Double-boxes are rare and must be given a special note. There are sixteen complete examples and 31 partial ones, and of these 47 which come from thirteen different sites, 21 have evidence of roller marking (examples from Eastbourne and London showing the use of two different rollers), while three are combed, two are scored, and five have a most unusual form of marking. This gives the impression of regular rows of rough pits about 10 mm in diameter.

These marks first suggested the use of a roller, but personal experiment has shown that they seem to have been dabbed on with the finger-tips. This odd marking is found only on tile from Wiggonholt, Angmering and Chichester, which suggests a common local source.

Some attempt has been made to analyse the various patterns of combing and there seem to be at least 80 identifiable patterns. The commonest is some form of cross, e.g. St Andrew's or saltire, or with additional lines, producing a Union Jack or variation of it. The straight line seems to be preferred to the curved or squiggled line which is found in only nineteen patterns, and would be more difficult to make. It is difficult to know whether these patterns represent the work of different groups of tile makers, whether they can be regarded as a form of signature or whether they merely express some whim of the maker. That a man did not always keep to one fixed pattern seems to be proved by the evidence on several examples of a different pattern being put on different faces, as with examples from Richborough and Springhead, both of which have a cross on one side and squiggles on the other.

Some sites have produced a quantity of box-tiles, and attempts have been made to analyse the types. Fifty examples from Darenth were noted to have four different designs, and they were thought to belong to different gangs or 'stools' of tile-makers at a factory with each gang having its own combing design as an identification. (Payne, 1897, 70). There may possibly have been some artistic urge to produce a distinctive pattern, and this could be a reason why such elaborate and decorative designs were produced when a quite simple one would have served the purpose just as efficiently.

Evidence from the kiln-site at Itchingfield suggested that the boxes were all of the cube type with no vents, and that two combs were used throughout. One had four teeth and a track of 27 mm, the other seven teeth and a track also of 27 mm. The user of the first indulged in free squigglings, while the second tended to keep to straight lines (Green, 1970, 32).

The Beauport Park collection has produced only nine complete box tiles – all scored, and an analysis of all fragments shows that while 70 per cent of all the box tiles used were of this scored type (in two sizes) the other 30 per cent provided seventeen different types of combing.

Though any attempt to identify a tile-maker from a pattern would be inconclusive, there are a few examples of box tile which show a definite individuality. On some of these the blank spaces on the face have been filled in in an unusual way. An example from Itchingfield has four sets of jab marks stabbed on with the end of a four-toothed comb; one from Havant has two bare panels between three sets of straight combings and one of these panels is filled with lines of squiggles, the other with a set of jab marks at 150 mm intervals. Five sites have examples of similar sets of jabs with a five-toothed comb, while those from Ashtead and Bignor have an elaborate form of little half-moons drawn in the gaps between the arms of the combing.

Fingers seem seldom to have been used to mark box-tiles, but an example from Fishbourne has squiggles and curves that are finger-made, as are also those from Bitterne and Newcastle. The best hand-marking evidence comes from Brading and from Binchester, where a number of complete box-tiles have on them the deliberate impression of a hand. In the making of modern hand-made roof tiles, the hand is sometimes used as a kind of suction to lift the soft tile from one place to another quite safely; the hand impressions still remain on these modern tiles, but the purpose just mentioned would not apply to Roman examples.

Scoring

Scoring is much less common than combing, and the often very thin knife-cuts cannot have provided much grip for keying. Scoring was certainly less sophisticated and less efficient than combing, and it might have been an earlier practice from which the use of the comb developed.

There are only two regular scoring patterns, lattice with diagonal lines, or straight lines producing rectangles. The sizes of the diamonds or rectangles very considerably, as does the thickness of the marking line. The Beauport Park examples have lines deeply incised with a knife and these are only 1 mm wide, but examples from Bletchley and Leicester have shallow lines as wide as 5 mm, made possibly with a stick. A variant is shown on a Gloucester example where the use of a stick 7 mm wide has created wavy lines which have odd-length endings which no comb could have produced.

Roller-printed relief patterns

Another form of marking is that made by engravings on a roller, similar to a modern paint roller. A.W.G. Lowther (1948) made a special study of such markings. A reappraisal has added 55 more examples (Johnston and Williams, 1979, 375–393), and still more are coming to light.

Here is a summary of Lowther's conclusions (1948, 10)

50 A roller-printed box tile from London

1 The relief pattern on flue tiles served the same purpose as that of
   the usual combed ones, and when the tiles were in use the pattern
   would have been covered with plaster, and not visible.

51 Roller-printed patterns on box-tile
a. Dog and Stag.
b. Florid (after Lowther)

2 Distribution implies a centre in the London area, but itinerant craftsmen travelled about the country from site to site taking their rollers with them, or perhaps lending them out.
3 Manufacture of relief-patterned tiles was confined to non-military sites, at which the craftsmen, paid probably according to output, would wish to have their work easily identified.
4 Evidence suggests 80–150 AD as the period in which the dies were originally in use. Re-use of tile makes their final date obscure.

Lowther listed nine groups broken down into 47 varieties covering 130 examples and with a few exceptions they came from the

52 Cabriabanus' advertisement on tile from Plaxtol (Scale ½)

south-east of Britain. Of these examples, three only were on voussoir and one on curved tile, the rest were on box tile.

Many of the relief-patterns were so elaborate and intricate that one wonders at the care taken over a pattern that seemed destined to be covered over with plaster – is it not just possible that some of the pictorial ones like the 'Dog and Stag' representation might have remained visible on box-tiles that were set lengthwise at the top of the wall to act as a sort of decorative dado or frieze? Another possible explanation is that the attractive patterns were made to please purchasers of boxes when they came to some builder's yard. The lettered relief pattern from Plaxtol (and a variant from Darenth) in which a certain Cabriabanus proclaimed his work must surely have been a sort of advertisement.

There are other combed or roller-printed examples not recorded by Lowther which show some lettered or pictorial evidence. These include :

a.   A fragment from Fishbourne which has the letter M filling a space between the combing.
b.   A complete box tile from London has the imprint PXTX repeated at top and bottom between lines of chevron. (Roach Smith, 1859, 114)
c.   A box from Ridgewell has the figure VI incorporated in the roller print.

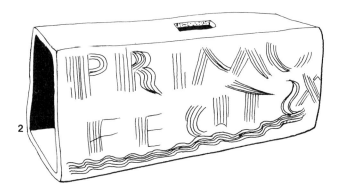

53. 1. Lettered roller marking on box-tile, London
    2. Graffito made with comb on box-tile, Leicester

d.   An example from Edington had the roller-print of a cross set above a circle, which is said to match a similar example from Leicester.

Other examples of letters or patterns imposed on box-tiles include :

e.   A large box-tile from Bignor has undecipherable letters scratched within a triangle on the side of the tile just above the vent.
f.   A box-tile from Stonesfield has two circles and a linking bar (resembling a pair of scissors) impressed over the combing.
g.   An example from Rapsley has a set of letters scratched in a gap between the combing just above the vent.
h.   A fragment from Canterbury has the letters MINUCI inscribed on the inside of the box.

Combed or scored brick

Some brick bears combing or scoring extensively all over the surface. Since this was primarily an aid to the attachment of mortar or plaster, it would be reasonable to find it on half-boxes or vertically-mounted wall tiles, but there seems little obvious need for it elsewhere. A number of examples of brick are scored in small squares, compared with the large squares or lattice scoring found on half-boxes. One reason for such scoring could be that the brick was intended for use as a gaming board (e.g. Ludus Duodecim Scriptorum). A complete one, measuring 480 mm × 430 mm × 10 mm was found at Holt (Bell, 1960, 31, fig.26). Three other sites have produced fragments of a similar board. Another possibility is that the brick was marked in squares either as imitation *tesserae* or scored perhaps as a preliminary to cutting up for *tesserae*. Examples come from nine sites.

Combing

There are some items in which the surface has been heavily combed into deep rills, as from Beauport Park, Bodiam, York, Dover, and Richborough. On most of these the body of the brick is salmon-coloured, and it has what seems to be a superimposed coating of a creamy buff colour, and it is on this surface that there is the distinctive deep rilling to create squares, diamonds, or curves. Four of the sites mentioned are Classis Britannica ones, and there are some fine examples to be seen in the Pharos at Dover.

Some of the finger-made markings to be seen on brick, e.g. from Templebrough and Castleford are so wide apart that it seems that the

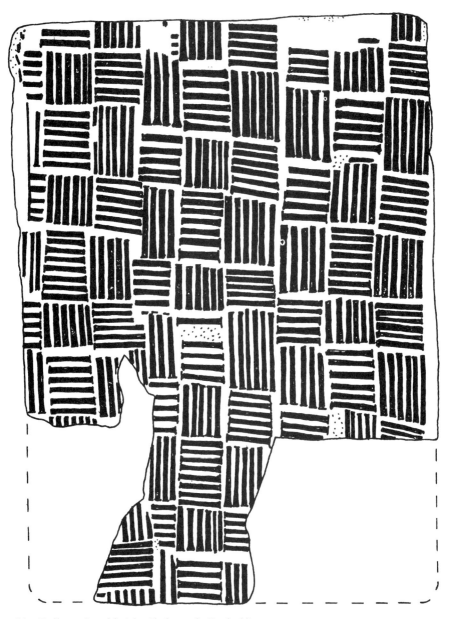

54 Roller-printed brick, Shakenoak (Scale ¼)

55   A varied selection of tile-stamps. (Scale ½)

purpose might have been not so much to act as rendering for mortar as to serve as an anti-slip device, especially if the brick was used to pave the floor. There is also a rare example from Chester of brick having grooves gouged out after firing, which might have had the same purpose.

There are several examples of brick which is covered with a widely spaced chevron pattern which seems to have been roller printed. Items come from Pulborough, Chanctonbury Ring, Angmering, Arundel, and Wiggonholt, and these may all have come from the same source, since the sites are not distant from each other, and similar marking is not found elsewhere. Shakenoak provides an almost complete roller printed brick; it measured 465 mm × 330 mm × 35 mm and though there were no nail-holes or notches, it could have been a wall-tile. It was covered all over with billet pattern Lowther No.25 (Brodribb *et al*, 1973, 40 and fig.21 (73)).

Tile Stamps

The purpose of stamping

The chief reason for putting a stamp on a tile is to show an identity. The samian potters put their names on their work, and so did makers of *mortaria* and *amphorae*. Makers of eye-salve labelled their goods as a form of advertisement. Silver ingots found in London carried an official stamp, which also appears on certain writing tablets, on leather, on barrels, and even on bread (like the present Hovis mark).

The military and naval departments concerned with the making of tile used stamps as a sign of their authority. It has been pointed out that the development of townships near the permanent Legionary Quarters increased the risk of theft from military stores, and created a need to apply proprietary marks (Boon, 1984, 16). The practice of marking official goods is still maintained to this day by bodies such as the Ministry of Defence, who in the past have used the broad arrow or the letters R.N. as their mark.

Private brick works would be more concerned with the use of a stamp for advertisement, and personal names appear, such as ARVERUS, PRIMUS, CANDIDUS, and CLEMENTINUS. They are sometimes put in the genitive case with an understood word such as *opus*, *officina*, or *manu*, i.e. the work of . . .

The earliest record of a stamped tile was probably that from York in 1706 (Wright, 1978, 382, iv.11). Little observation was made of others until the Rev. John Lyon discovered at Dover in 1778 a stamp bearing the letters CL BR (1779, 330). Though he was not correct in his interpretation of them, he was right in assuming that the letters represented some official body or unit. Subsequent evidence showed that it was customary for military forces, Legions, Cohorts, and Auxiliaries, as well as the Romano-British navy, the Classis Britannica, to put stamps upon tile.

On the continent the earliest Legionary stamps date back to about AD 43, but the practice of stamping in Britain came later. The earliest military building in Britain using brick and tile is the Legio II bath-house at Exeter (AD 60–65), but no stamped tile has been found there, and little stamped legionary tile in Britain can be positively dated to the first century (Boon, 1984, 15). The various legions in Britain started stamping their tiles at different times and the general practice of stamping must belong to the mid-second century. Of the auxiliary units that stamped tiles, the majority belong to the third century (Hassall, 1979, 261–6, and McWhirr, 1979, 253–9).

At the same time other official bodies put stamps on their tiles. Tile found in London carried the letters PP BR LON (with some variations). The letters stand for '*Provinciae Britanniae Londonii*', i.e. 'of the province of Britain at Londinium'; and the first P stands probably for '*procurator*', who would have had headquarters in London and been responsible for public buildings.

The colonia at Gloucester had its own municipal tilery with stamps marked RPG (*Rei publicae Glevensium*), and no doubt other stamps have some official connection. There were also private tileries who stamped their tiles. Among these are interesting examples of stamps which have a different letter added to the three initial letters, e.g. the T P F series from Gloucestershire or the LVL series from Lincoln which are found with an additional fourth letter, e.g. LVL-A, LVL-D.

The last letter could possibly refer to a particular branch of the tilery which produced them, or even the particular man. At the present time in a tilery at Keymer in Sussex, each tile bears the stamp 'Keymer' followed by various letters. This single letter shows from which bench each tile came, since each bench had its own metal stamp with an integrated different letter; so every tile could for ever be identified with a particular bench.

The stamping implement

Dies for stamps seem to have been made out of several different materials.

i   *Wood*   The evidence for this is signs of grain being visible in
     many impressions, e.g. a very good one of a Legio II stamp
     from the amphitheatre at Caerleon (Boon, 1980, 15). Dies cut on
     the end-grain of a piece of timber produce better impressions
     than those cut from side grain timber. The presence of a handle
     attached to some dies is proved by a nail-head mark damaging
     the letters of some examples of CL BR stamps (Brodribb, type I
     B), where the nail has not been driven in far enough and stands
     proud. In other examples (type I C) the nail has been driven in
     too far, leaving an indentation on the face. Similar evidence of a
     mark made by a nail head occurs on a Legio II stamp (Boon,
     1984, 17).
     Objection to dies being made of wood lies in the tendency of
     letters to wear or break off, and also the need of the tile makers
     to call on outside help from a wood carver. Unless there are the
     exceptional circumstances of sealing under damp conditions,
     such as those which have lead to the finding of wooden writing
     tablets (e.g. at Vindolanda), dies made of wood have little
     chance of survival.

ii   *Clay*   This would be readily available to tile makers, and
     personal experiment has shown that baked clay dies, with an
     integrated handle needing no attachment, make good impres-
     sions. There is evidence of clay dies being used for other objects
     e.g. the stamp for *mortaria* in the museum at Cambridge. In 1981
     a rectangular ceramic stamp was found in the barracks area at
     Chester, measuring 108 × 62 mm and 20 mm thick. The
     stumps of a double-looped handle appear on the back. (Brit XV,
     1984, 342, (17) and pl. XXV)

iii *Metal*   Some impressions are so sharp and clean-cut that they
     seem to have been made by some metal object, though no metal
     dies concerning Romano-British material have been found. It is
     possible that dies were deliberately destroyed when no longer
     required in order to avoid misuse of them. There is however in
     the Museum of London an iron die that makes the letters M P
     BR (*Metalla Prov. Brit.*) and could have been used on soft metal
     such as lead (Merrifield, 1969, 72). Other metal dies not directly
     linked with known impressions have been found, e.g. at Caer-
     leon and at Chester, where in the Grosvenor Museum there is a
     stamp made of lead. Legionary stamps made of lead have also
     been found (Boon, 1984, 17).
     In the Cambridge University Museum there are five bronze
     dies, but they seem to have no association with Roman Britain,

and have no known provenance. On all of these the letters stand out in relief from the face of the die, creating indented impressions. The type is unusual; on almost all the CL BR stamps the lettering stands out in relief, and it is the same with most legionary stamps. To produce a correct impression the die has to be cut in reverse, but sometimes the cutter of a new die has mistakenly copied direct from a stamp on a tile, and as a result the new stamp has come out retrograde. On a few stamps, e.g. from Benwell and Lincoln, the letters may have been put on individually with a kind of punch, making deep impressions.

iv   Letters have been marked on with a pointed implement such as a stick. Such examples, e.g. the letters VV from Melandra Castle, are rare (Hopkinson, 1906, 93–5), but there are some Fleet stamps which read C B.

v   There are a few examples of letters being written on by hand, e.g. of Legio II (McWhirr, 1979, 253), and sometimes a single finger-written letter may have had the same purpose as a stamp, e.g. the letter R from Combley (Fennelly, 1969, 281).

There is one unique oddity in a stamp of Neronian date found near Silchester; in the stamping a piece of thin fabric has been placed between the die and the tile, slightly smudging the impression. The purpose may have been to preserve the face of the die (Greenaway, 1981, 290–1).

The size and shape of stamps

The size of stamps varies considerably: they are usually oblong, and among CL BR examples the area of the stamp ranges from the smallest of 420 mm^2 (35 mm × 12 mm deep) to the largest (from Boulogne) of 5075 mm^2 (145 mm wide × 35 mm deep). The position of the stamp is usually central but the angle of imposition is very haphazard. There are also circular and oval stamps, and a few square ones.

The letters are usually surrounded by a clear-cut frame, and some legionary stamps (but only one CL BR one) are ansate, i.e. they have a sideways-on V-shaped pattern at each end, forming the shape of a handle (*ansa*).

None of the stamps are as comprehensively lettered as the circular Imperial brick-stamps found in Rome and elsewhere, with their characteristic disc-shaped bite (*orbilicus*) out of the edge. Sometimes the stamper has used his die twice on the same tile. In most cases the

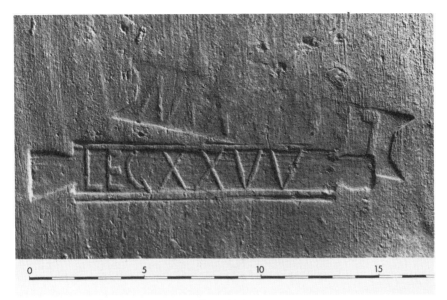

56 Overprinted Legionary Stamp from Holt

second stamping seems to have been imposed not because the first was too indefinite, but simply at the whim of the stamper.

Some of these multiple stamps overlap: one tile from Dover has as many as three impressions imposed almost on top of each other, while an *imbrex* from Caerleon has three stamps separately imposed upon it, as though it was an experimental stamping. It does not appear again except in a shorter version. There is one unique stamping from Holt where a *tegula* has a worn fish-tail stamp overprinted by an unworn ansate stamp. (Boon, 1984, 15 & pl.6 a)

Such curiosities must have a tale to tell. At Beauport Park one *imbrex* has a signature 'cancelled' by a stamp on top (all Beauport Park *imbrices* have either a stamp or a signature, but not both). It is also possible from some Beauport Park stamps to identify characteristics of the stamper, e.g. the man who puts his stamp always in a particular position.

There is one example of stamping unique in that it has been made on the outside of the flange instead of on the face, and the stamp has been incorporated into the tile mould itself. Parts of five possible stamps have been found on *tegulae* fragments from Stanton Low. None of the stamps was complete, but there are two varieties, one

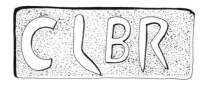

57   The most ubiquitous of all CLBR stamps – possibly the prototype. (Scale ½)

bearing the name AVIENUS, while the other takes the form of a St Andrew's Cross with a frame almost as deep as the flange (Jones, 1981, 336). The stamps are in positive relief, and each type shows variations of die. The position in which these stamps have been imposed would preclude them from being easily seen.

The variety of stamp types

There is a very wide variety of stamp suggesting that new dies were constantly in demand. The evidence of CL BR stamps from Britain shows that there are some 120 different varieties of die from the total of 2338 stamps so far published (Brodribb, 1980). Quantities are most variable, ranging from 495 examples (type 1), down to only one, of which there are as many as 62. From Beauport Park alone there are no less than 23 unique examples out of a total number of 56 varieties, which is very puzzling.

The evidence of Legionary stamps is much slighter, but Wright's two surveys (1976, 224–235 and 1978, 379–382) shows 79 varieties out of 235 examples of Legio VI stamps, and fifteen varieties out of 97 stamps of Legio IX. It seems possible that there was a prototype CL BR stamp, since one stamp (Brodribb type 1) appears on as many as seven out of the ten CL BR British sites. Later, the makers of dies seem to have been given a free hand in their design. Many varieties differ only very slightly, as though a die had been re-cut or inaccurately copied. Shrinkage through firing also accounts for some small difference in size. One stamp formed of two panels was broken down the middle, but one half went on being used as a stamp (Brodribb type 20J). Obvious flaws in cutting produced most helpful evidence in identification.

The question arises whether certain stamps tended to be confined to certain types of tile: evidence from CL BR stamps from Beauport Park suggests that this was so, as this table will show.

Stamp type number	Tegulae	Imbrices	Brick of all kinds	Total
1	95	5	10	110
2		109		109
20	198		14	212
25	194		30	224
27	1	62		63
28		81		81
29	2	148		150

It would be interesting to know the reason for the 'odd men out' examples.

It is not yet possible to do a complete breakdown for the material from Boulogne, but the range of varieties seems very wide. There are several types common to both Britain and Boulogne, showing that there was some cross-Channel exchange of production.

The CL BR stamps can be given no firmer dating than that they were in production between the early second century and the mid-third century.

One 'famous' stamp from Pevensey reading HON AUG ANDRIA supposedly gave evidence for the restoring of defences during Emperor Honorius' reign (395–423 AD) but after appearing for many years in numerous publications since the first finding in 1902, the stamp was proved to be a fake seventy years later, having some connection with Charles Dawson, who may have been concerned with the Piltdown forgery (Peacock, 1973, 138–40). In the Museum of London there is another forged stamp reading VNDINIC (Cuming, 1869, 391).

The frequency of use

It would be interesting to know whether stamps were impressed on every tile or only on a selected few. Evidence from Beauport park tile shows that out of 41 complete *tegulae* only one failed to carry a stamp, suggesting that stamping throughout was usually intended. Unfortunately no other site gives much evidence on the matter, though of the 57 complete *tegulae* used to create tile tombs at York, 36 carried stamps (30 of Legio VI, and six of Legio IX); and of the ten complete *imbrices* concerned, only five produced stamps, four of Legio VI and one of Legio IX. (Pers. comm. I.M. Betts) Over 150 stamps were found in the Fortress Baths at Caerleon, though the number of tiles used would have been many times greater. It has been pointed out that many of the tiles may have been old ones made at a time before stamping was common; and the total of newer stamped ones would have become diluted among the many reused old ones (Boon, 1980, 2). One particular consignment of tile used at Brecon Gaer may possibly have been stamped throughout (Wheeler, 1926, 10).

Over the wide time-range of tile stamping in Britain, one cannot expect an entirely uniform practice, and it may simply be that some units were more particular over their stamping than others, and that some tiles were carelessly neglected, whatever the regulations may have been. It always seems strange that where one stamp has been found on a site, there are not always a great many others.

Of the 461 sites which have produced material for the Survey only 64 provided stamped tiles, nine CL BR, 27 military and 28 others.

While attempting to establish the proportions of stamps on different types of tile, little evidence among Legionary stamped tile was found, but it is possible to provide some facts concerning CL BR material. Of the 2338 CL BR stamps in Britain so far published, the quantity of various types on which they appear works out as follows:

Tegulae	765
Imbrices	830
Brick (all sizes)	670
Box-flue	38

(there are also 35 unidentified examples)

These totals are dominated by the quantity of 1333 stamps from Beauport Park and 814 from Dover, but between these two sites there is a great discrepancy of types as this table shows:

	Beauport Park	Dover
Tegulae	722	43
Imbrices	580	250
Brick	175	480
Box flue	3	26

A possible reason for this may be that the site at Beauport Park is a small bath house, with roofing requiring some 1100 *tegulae*, little need for brick, and with most of the floors intact, while the material from Dover covered a wide area of fortress remains including walls that may have had bonding tile.

It is clear from evidence that where stamping occurs the *tegulae* is the most likely tile to be stamped, and that larger brick is more likely to be stamped than small *bessales*. At Beauport Park for example, not a single one of the 79 complete *bessales* recovered from only carried a stamp, and stamps on box-tile are very rare, which is odd for a tile that required some skill in making; only 38 examples come from the 2338 CL BR stamps listed, and this slender proportion is confirmed by Wright's analysis of stamps of Legio VI and IX. This shows that only two out of the 333 examples were made on box-flue. No stamp has been found on hollow voussoirs, but there has been the odd stamp on cornice bricks (Caerleon) and a plinth (Boulogne).

A select bibliography of material concerned with stamped tile will be found after the general bibliography.

Impressions and Imprints

Before a new tile was fully dry and ready to be fired, it provided a surface that would easily take any impression imposed upon it. Official stamping has already been discussed, but there are other forms of impression to be considered.

The handling of tile in its plastic state has often resulted in finger marks, e.g. at the point of balance of *imbrices*, and finger prints are sometimes clear enough to suggest the fanciful idea of trying to identify the tile maker from his prints, but evidence would be too scanty. It was while the tile was being left out to dry that impressions were made by humans as well as animals. There are prints of bare feet of all sizes, and there are prints of sandals and heavier boots showing a complete set of studs, and these help our knowledge of Roman footwear. Some footprints were submitted to the Chelsea School of Chiropody and the formation and spread of the toes shows the feet to be in perfect natural state seldom found today.

The prints made by wandering animals show a wide variety of creatures such as dog, cat, sheep, goat, deer, pig, horse, cow, badger, wolf and bird. The very rare prints on *imbrices* are all claw marks made on the edge of the imbrex as though a dog had reached up to the tile drying on a raised rack, a possible clue about tile production.

Other unusual prints include those of what must be raindrops, only found from four sites, and the rarity suggests that tile was usually kept under cover, perhaps in open-sided sheds. There are at least ten imprints of textile material, and a tile from Lullingstone shows where the cloth had been forced in by a cow stamping on it. Such prints often provide enough evidence for the type of material to be identified. Occasionally there are imprints on the underside of the tile – these include one of a fern leaf and a clump of grasses.

Sometimes there are deep regular channels crossing the underside of the tile as though it has rested on some sort of rack or frame to lift it off the ground.

One very unusual imprint on the reverse side of a tile from Piddington shows the clear imprint of some *tesserae* of a mosaic floor on which presumably the tile had been laid for drying. The *tesserae* were large (25 mm × 20 mm) and match those making up floors at Piddington, suggesting that these imprinted tiles were made on site (Pers. comm. R. M. Friendship-Taylor).

It is always worth while looking at the underside of a tile; some are very cleanly smoothed off, others left very rough and sometimes with the traces of sand on which they had been lying. This smoothing of some surfaces was part of the process. We have a cryptic graffito scratched *in magna tegula* from Aquileia (CIL V, 8110, 968) which reads:

> Cave malum si non raseris lateres DC: si raseris minus, malum formidabis.

This could be freely translated as 'Watch out carefully and see that you do not fail to scrape (those) 600 bricks: if you deal with less than that, you will have good reason to feel afraid (of the consequences)'. But there are problems about this: 600 would far exceed the norm of about 200 bricks for a man's daily production, unless he was confined simply to scraping the surface in the manner in which a man would apply a comb to a box-tile, but *lateres* would scarcely require any combing. It looks as if *raseris* must concern something more technical than 'scraping'.

Some of the animal prints are very deep, almost penetrating the tile (e.g. a hoof mark from Reculver). Animal-printed tile has usually attracted the interest of past excavators who otherwise ignored tile, and in some museums it is the only tile on show. No full study of animal prints has yet been made, but it would tell us much about the fauna of Romano-British times. Cram and Fulford (1979, 201–209) have, however, made some study of faunal prints on tile from Silchester, and the thirteen tons of tile so far analysed from Beauport Park include 163 examples of prints showing eight studded marks, fifteen by bare feet, 88 by dogs, 22 by cats, twelve by sheep or goat, ten by other cloven prints, three each by small mammals and birds, and one each by horse and piglet. One tile shows a large cloven print with a very small one beside it, possibly made by a sheep with its lamb.

There have also been a number of unofficial casual imprints including a tile-comb from Beauport Park, (see section on markings), a circular imprint with indented holes (Gayton Thorpe), wheel-shaped impressions and imprint of a buckle or clasp (both from Silchester), and that of a coin with the letters SC (*Senatus consultu*) evident from Richborough.

There are also several very different kinds of impressions which have information to give, such as chunks of mortar bearing impressions of tile and masonry showing their relative positions. From Godmanchester there is a piece of Torching (i.e. mortar filling) from *imbrices* on the ridge and also some end fillings of the lowest course of *imbrex* showing impressions of other tiles (Green, 1959, 254). From Well there is a piece of mortar 200 mm thick which shows impressions of three box-flues which have been set flush side by side with no mortar between them (Gilyard-Beer, 1951, 67). From Wiggonholt a similar mortar impression shows the relationship between several voussoirs.

Graffiti

The still soft surface of a new tile must have seemed to the tilemaker almost to offer an invitation for something to be scratched upon it. Graffiti on tile has in general been well covered by Tomlin (1979, 231–251), but it is relevant to mention here a few examples which relate to tile by name or implication. The interpretation of a graffito is often difficult, but the examples given below all suggest that the tile-maker has something he wishes to say about his work.

Graffiti	Tile	Site	Reference
Tubulus			
TVBL	on *tubulus*	Barnsley Park	Corinium Museum
(TVBVL) OS XDL F . .	on 'building tile'	Dover	Britannia 4, 1973, 332
QVASSIAVI LI			
PRIMVS FECIT X	on *tubulus*	Leicester	EE, VII, 1143
FECIT TVBVL	on *tubulus*	Silchester	EE, IX, 1292 B
CLEMENTINVS			
Tegula			
CAN(D)IDVS F (TEG)	on brick	Cirencester	Britannia 8, 1977, 439
VL			
(TE)G(UL)A		Willowford	J Roman Stud 37, 1947 (15), 182

58   Two important graffiti
    Top. 1.   Wiggonholt. (Scale ⅓)
    Bottom. 2.   Holt. (Scale ⅜)
    Trans. 'Iulius Aventinus soldier of the first cohort of the Sunici.'

Graffiti	Tile	Site	Reference
Pedalis			
PED		Colchester	Colchester Museum
ATTI PED	on *tegula*	Farningham	J Roman Stud 55
		(Franks Hall)	1965 (28), 226
XX FIICI		Tomen Y Muir	J Roman Stud 38
			1948 (18), 103
P(ILARES) XX	on *bessalis*	Wiggonholt	J Roman Stud 30
CUNATI IIII			1940 (20), 188
TVBV (LI)N DLX			

Another tile-making reference already mentioned is Cabriabanus'
claim to be a maker of *parietalis* (wall-tile). Some comments are
casual recordings of satisfaction at work achieved. A self-congratula-

59 Graffiti a. London (Scale ¼)
      b. Hartfield (Scale ½)
      c. Silchester (Scale ⅛)

60   Graffito of a Pharos-like building, London

tory graffito on a tile from Wymbush (Bucks.) wishes 'good health
to us . . . three who made this tile' (Britannia 11, 1980, 407 no.9).
There is also the laconic but expressive comment of 'SATIS'
scratched with a finger on a tile from Silchester (EE IX 1292 c), and
comments on tiles from Siscia (Pannonia) give some idea of a
tile-maker's total for a day's work. One (CIL, III, 11383) states that
two named workmen between them made 440 tiles on July 28, and
another (CIL III, 11381) tells how four workmen (also named) each
made 220 tiles on July 1. From Britain comes a graffito from Hartfield
which gives the numbers 220 and 214 – a day's tally for two workers.
(Britannia 16, 1985, 327): the number 220 also appears on a tile from
Heybridge (Britannia, 13, 1982, 411), and a dated tile from London
suggests a total of 225 (Britannia, 11, 1980, 413). Another tile from
Silchester (EE IX 1294) gives a day's score of 199, as well as a date –

September 26. Other graffito giving dates include the tile from London just mentioned – a date early in August, and one from Caerleon gives the date July 25.

But even such scanty information can suggest the probable output for a day's work, and the dates also show that tile-making, at least in the more northern parts of the Empire, may have been confined to the summer months. Vitruvius (II, 3, 2) stated that the proper time for tile-making in Italy was the spring and autumn, the summer being too hot for consistent baking.

Another form of graffito is that of the pictorial kind, and one of the most interesting of these must be the drawing on a *bessalis* tile from London which comes from the Roach Smith collection. It seems to be an impression of a Pharos-like building.

The Tally-mark

Some seventy years ago in his report on excavations at Gelligaer Ward commented: 'The bricks were remarkably fine and well-shaped, of uniform texture and thicker than usual and were scored with an X on one edge' (1909, 40). This must surely be the first Romano-British reference to a marking that is now usually referred to as a 'TALLY-MARK', since many of these marks appear to be numerical, and may have something to do with the reckoning of quantities or batches of tile. The next reference to a tally-mark comes in a note on a CL BR stamped tile from Dover which 'carried the numeral IV on its edge'. (Amos, 1921, 239, item 13).

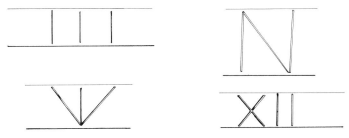

61   Four varieties of tally-mark – Beauport Park. (Scale ⅜)

In the following year in his report on the fort at Templebrough, May referred to a two-inch thick brick 'that had the number IV inscribed before baking' (1922, 122). A more detailed reference later came from Newstead and Droop in a report on excavations at Chester in 1935. This reads: 'Roof tiles with stamps have numerals cut on the edge. The first two (Nos. 10 & 11) are on type 3 stamps and seem to read VI and III. No.12 has numerals IIX or XII, and no.13 may read V or II. These marks all occupying the relative position, are puzzling, but it is possible if not probable that they may represent tile-makers' marks' (1936, 43 and plate XXI, items 10–13).

At Beauport Park (Brodribb, 1979, 139–150) numerous examples of marks were discovered cut on the fore-edge of *tegulae* and the edges of brick, but none on *imbrex*, box-flue or voussoir. The record so far amounts to 256 examples, 155 on *tegulae*, and 101 on various forms of brick. A breakdown of these marks shows that there were some twenty different types, some appearing more frequently than others, and though brick was less commonly found than *tegula*, it seemed more likely to carry a tally-mark. This evidence is supported from other sites.

Of the 41 complete *tegulae* found so far at Beauport Park sixteen carried tally-marks, there were thirteen on the 72 complete *bessales* found while five of the thirteen large floor tiles lifted for inspection had them. This produced a total of 34 out of 126 complete examples, or about one in four, but this cannot be regarded as a general guide since some types of *tegulae*, e.g. those with type 5 signature (32 examples), and those with a type 25 CL BR stamp (22 examples) never carried a tally-mark. The Beauport Park tile collection has examples of *tegula* and brick which carry all three of the distinctive features, i.e. stamp, signature and tally-mark.

In a search for examples from othere sites, it soon became evident that six of the other sites at which CL BR stamps have been found produced 25 examples of tally-marks, and it first seemed that this might be a practice confined to Fleet sites. Further evidence however came from some military sites as well, e.g. Templebrough, Holt, Lancaster, Gelligaer, Caerleon, Colchester, Chester, Ribchester, and York which all produced positive though scanty evidence, though there was nothing from sites on Hadrian's Wall.

There are also single examples only from eight other sites : Chichester, Garden Hill, Layer de la Haye, London, Silchester, Slonk Hill, Verulamium, and Wendens Ambo. Excluding the many Beauport Park examples, those from elsewhere cover 23 sites, producing a total of 60 examples of tally-mark (31 on brick, 28 on *tegulae*, and one on imbrex (a possible ridge-tile). Though the overall quantity is small, there is a wide range of as many as 22 different types, the mark X being the commonest with nine examples. The mark IV near the apex of the fore-edge of an imbrex from Holt is unique in position, as is also the mark I I I on the outside of the flange of a *tegula* from Layer de la Haye.

It would be unreasonable to suppose that tally marking was a practice confined to Britain and in a 'sighting' contemporaneous with Ward's report on Gelligaer, Jahn in his report on Vindonissa (1909, 121) told of the finding of a combination of the marks 1, V, and X on the edge of tile, the highest figure amounting to XXI. All of the figures read the same both in upright and inverted position. There is another brief reference to such marking on tile from the Bas-Dauphiné area of France. This concerns the marks I and X, and the writer regarded them as 'marques de stockage' having no connection with Legionary numbers (Chauffin, 1956, 85).

A very unusual form of marking was found on tiles from Medes (France) which were once part of a ship's cargo. Near the lowest part of the face of some *tegulae*, but not on the fore-edge or within the area of the semicircular signature, were various finger-made marks taking the form of a V, a triangle, or two large dots. Cazzare regards them as 'marques de tacheron', a foreman's mark with possibly the same purpose as a tally-mark (Cazzare, 1976, 29). A possible Romano-British parallel to these marks are the finger-made dots – one, two or three in quantity on the apex of certain wide *imbrices* from Newport, I.O.W., which if they are not signatures, are almost the only examples of tally-marks found on an *imbrex* (Tomalin, 1975, 13).

Classification of the marks is difficult because:
1. Some numbers can be read the same either way up.
2. Slanting lines may really be vertical ones put on carelessly.
3. Some lines are mis-cut or poorly aligned.
4. The X mark is sometimes found set centrally, but sometimes at both ends of the fore-edge.

The first impression is that the marks represent Roman numerals. The single, double, triple and quadruple lines whether vertical or slanting seem to stand for 1, 2, 3, 4, and IIII for 4 is as common on inscriptions as IV. Similarly, on inscriptions VIIII is as common as IX. Figure N, one of the commonest marks, could perhaps stand for 4 even though the second line of the V is vertical, and it is possible to imagine Ψ – the V with a vertical line inserted in the middle – as representing 6. V could be a Roman V and could be found inverted.

The mark from Chichester which reads XΛ (or possibly VX) with the V oddly preceding the X, appears unusual, but may have been written retrograde, as in the graffito from Colchester which is mentioned later.

There seems to be an absence of any mark representing the numbers 7, 8 and 9, and there are several other marks that are obscure. If carelessly written handwriting can often produce confusion, it is not surprising that a mark cut with a knife can be difficult to recognise. But if Ѵ is not really a 6 and is another form of 4, then the whole series of 6–9 is missing – perhaps such figures were not required for a purpose which needed the figures 1–5 and then went on to 10. If the marks were not intended to be numerals then they must be symbols (cf. the 'secret marks on antique-dealers' price labels), but symbols must represent something to have a meaning, and it seems odd that some should follow the form of an ordinary numeral.

There are some examples of marking with multiple figures extended in such a way that they cannot be included among the above types. Some may possibly come into the category of those graffiti which refer to a tile-maker's activity.

1.   In 1942 an unusual marking was found on the edge of a tile in the city wall at Verulamium, it reads: IIII III III IIS, with diagonal strokes across each group. A report says: 'It appears to be a tile-maker's score. If the stroke that erases each group of numerals is not regarded as an additional number, and the final mark is taken for a flourish rather than an S for S (emis), the total will be 12 batches or groups to be handled.' (Dunning and Corder, 1943, 80, item 11).

2.   Another similar extended number was noticed in 1938 on the edge of a brick in the first bastion to the north of the Balkerne Gate, Colchester: it is still *in situ*. This retrograde mark reads: I I I V X I. The note suggests, 'It is apparently a tile-maker's score of 68, and cannot be related to any Legion' (J Roman Stud 34 (1944) 90, item 17).

62   Multiple tally-mark from Colchester on brick still in situ (Scale ½)

3.   A *Lydion* brick from Boulogne has on one edge five vertical strokes with a spacing of 80 mm between Nos. 2 and 3 and 3 and 4, the whole marking covering a length of 220 mm.

4.   A *sesquipedalis* brick from Beauport Park, of which three-

quarters survives, has markings on two of its edges. One edge has three vertical strokes and round the corner on an adjacent edge is a marking composed of four sloping strokes, with an interval of 80 mm between the two pairs; there are also five other faintly marked curved strokes scattered in between.

The meaning of the marks

Any search for the meaning of tally-marks on tile must consider similar forms of marking found on pottery. A full survey of pottery marking with special reference to that from Mucking suggests that some of those marks seem to resemble Roman numerals (M.V. Jones, 1972, 335–38). Cunliffe records marks found amongst the considerable amount of pottery from Fishbourne as 'batch-marks' or 'batch-numerals' (1971, 108 *et alia*). Similar marks were found on pottery at other sites in West Sussex, and these often seemed to represent numbers. In a report these are also labelled as 'batch-marks', scratched on just below the rim with a sharp tool before firing (Hodder, 1974a, 86 and fig.1).

It is one thing to speak of 'batch-marks' and another matter to say exactly what this term means, and since we do not know what proportion of pots carried them, we cannot be certain if they were put on only occasionally to represent a particular batch of pots made, or perhaps to signify the end of a work period. The wide range of different marks must have had some scheme.

Other possible parallels have been considered. There is a current practice at the Keymer tile works in which the tile at the top of a stack is marked to show where the next counting starts from, and so records each batch. Also at the Keymer works a brickmaker stated that when he joined the works and had finished his apprenticeship, he was allotted a personal number (e.g. 10), and that number stayed with him in his work permanently, so that any production of his could always be identified.

There is possibly another analogy. It seems that in times past carpenters used to mark wood on each component of a framed building in order to identify its position. 'The carpenter used a coding system . . . all the numerals were additive to avoid mistakes caused by reading the mark upside down. So 4 was written as IIII; VI and IV always mean 6, XI and IX always mean 11. A stroke could be saved by writing 15 as X/and 20 as X' (McCann, 1982). There is a parallel with the tile in the way in which numbers could be read either way up.

CHAPTER 6

COLOUR, FABRIC, AND TEXTURE

The subject of the clay fabric of brick and tile is highly complex. Difference in fabric can be identified provisionally under the hand lens, but when examined under a microscope the differences become more acute, and it needs a skilled eye to identify these. Almost every site provided more than one type of fabric, some as many as twenty types, but since there is not yet any common standard by which they can be judged or any catalogue of fabric types to which they can be referred, comparisons can be meaningless. The matter is complicated by more than one type of fabric coming from the same clay pit as modern tileries confirm. All that can safely be said is there are a great number of identifiable types of clay to be found on Romano-British sites and perhaps one day there may be a code by which they can be labelled.

The original source of clay would certainly be of interest where fabric from one site seems to match that from another. There is already evidence of tile being made with clay from France being found in Britain and vice-versa.

Fabric must never be confused with colour. An observation of any quantity of tile and brick will show that while it is usually red in colour there are variations that range from white, cream, yellow, buff, pink, orange, red, crimson, brown, mauve, grey, blue, and even black. The way in which such changes of colour come about has been well explained (Davey, 1961, 65).

Tile of orange colour often has a surface that tends to rub off and stain the water and hands when the tile is washed. Tile can usually be scrubbed hard with no ill-effect, hence the old Latin tag about it being a waste of time 'lavare laterem' (*to wash tile*) (Terence, Phormio I,4.9).

In another comment on colour it was stated that a few yellow tiles found at Park Street, St Albans and frequently in London 'were made

136

from clay containing up to 8% of chalk either occurring naturally or being added to artificially'. (Davey, 1945, 106)

Though the quantities were irregular, this variety of colour gave some opportunity of experimenting with polychromatic effects. Tombs built wholly of brick of Hadrian's time show the use of variegated brick, as for example, that known as Deus Rediculus at the Porta San Sebastiano at Rome, where red tile is used for architectural features and yellow bricks for the walls. The guard house of the seventh cohort of Vigiles, and the amphitheatrum castrense on the Aurelian wall also show polychromatic design (Walters, 1905, 336).

In Britain such design is rare, but in the debris at Keston there was a quantity of white and red tiles (Fox, 1955, 105), and at Lullingstone there is a suggestion of "a gaily coloured roof with lines of yellow tiles alternating with the usual deep red" (Meates, 1955, 96). The same effect is claimed for a roof and wall in Lower Thames Street, London (Lethaby, 1923, 15 and Roach Smith, 1845, 114). A sporadic use of yellow brick "a feature of early 2nd century" was found at Verulamium (Wheeler, 1936, 141). It is reported that at Gadebridge Park 'Building A must have appeared garish as the roof was covered with red and yellow tiles' (Neal, 1974, 19). It is possible today to see in Mediterranean areas roofing made up of yellow, pink and red tile that gives a most pleasing effect.

It seems perhaps that the pale yellow coloured tile was sometimes regarded as undesirable and some yellow tiles found at Verulamium were deliberately painted red to make them appear the usual tile colour (Lowther, 1937, 36). It may well be that the painting of tiles was not uncommon, but time and exposure have usually caused the applied colour to vanish. There is however a group of Midland sites which provide definite evidence: these sites are Piddington, Peterborough, Lavendon, Bancroft, Towcaster, Stonea and Wood Corner, and they have all produced some *tegulae* and *imbrices* that are coloured with a variety of black, brown, maroon, scarlet or cream wash or slip. On one complete *tegula* from Bancroft a straight margin of paint is marked externally along the centre of the inverted flange, suggesting that the *tegula* was dipped reverse side up into a tray of wash deep enough to cover the whole face of the *tegula* and half of the flange.

Though the colour of the tile is little guide to the nature of its fabric, the feel of its texture is more revealing. Many tiles are sandy on the underside because they were dried on a sandy bed, but some are notably sandy on the top surface as well; other surfaces can be 'soapy' or very hard and shiny. Though it is common to find good quality *tegulae* with a cleaned-off underside, it is seldom as smooth as on the face, though some solid voussoir have both faces equally smooth. Sometimes brick can be found with combing on one side, and a very clean face on the other. Such smoothness must not be confused with that of a tile which has become worn through use in a doorway or passage.

Other oddities of surface are occasional blisters found on the face of the tile caused perhaps in the firing. From Beauport Park there are nine examples of *bessales* on which in the area of the stamp there are a number of fine pitted holes. It first seemed as if they were the result of some very small object like grit or seed having disintegrated, but tests have shown that they were very small craters where a bubble had burst. The cause is obscure, but they have been mentioned here to emphasise the wide range of items that close investigation of tile can produce.

An increasing number of reports contain some reference to fabric, and where the study is concentrated on some particular line, e.g. stamped tile or relief-patterned tile, it can be most informative. D.P.S. Peacock's analysis of tiles of the Classis Britannica is a notable example (1977, 235–248).

CHAPTER 7

PRODUCTION, DISTRIBUTION AND DATING

This study of tile shows that there were numerous types whose function in a building can be identified; a much wider problem is to know where the tile was made and how it was distributed. Only about 45 tile-making kilns have so far been recorded, which is extremely few for the amount of tile once produced (Darvill & McWhirr, 1984, 244, fig.3). With such scanty evidence it is reasonable to consider the practices of other times and places, and though this may not prove what was done in Roman Britain, it may suggest possibilities which can be tested against Roman evidence. To quote Peacock : 'If we wish to know how *imbrices* were made, we cannot do better than look at present production in Sicily'. (1979, 5 etc.) He goes on to suggest several categories in production, and these are summarised here with thanks to him:

1. Household production of bricks for private consumption.
2. Small rural brickyards employing enough men to supply the needs of a local area. This has been a common practice all over the world, and avoids the considerable cost of transport.
3. Brick-making in N.W. Europe is traditionally seasonal, and could be linked with farming. Skilled workers could be mobile and surface clamp kilns could be erected on site by itinerant brick-makers.
4. Complexes of brick-yards springing up round an area where there is an abundant supply of fine quality clay. These must be populated areas where there is high demand.
5. Estate brickworks which could market bricks surplus to the needs of the estate. (Possibly kilns at Eccles and Ashstead were of this kind.)
6. Municipal brickworks run by local authorities. The tiles stamped R P G (Rei publicae Glevensis) and tiles stamped PP BR LON are evidence of such official administration.

7. Brickworks of military or naval association such as the Legionary site at Holt and at Brampton (auxiliary), and that which supplied the *Classis Britannica*.

Peacock also supplied details of post-Roman parallels for these categories, and points out that the subject has never been studied seriously, and that most previous work on kilns has concentrated on kiln structure without being able to assess the nature of the works or buildings which must have been associated with the kiln, two exceptions being the studies of the works at Holt (Grimes, 1930), and at Itchingfield (Green, 1970 and 1979).

McWhirr (1979, 97–189) has listed the evidence of tile-kilns found in Britain, and it surprisingly shows that the majority of civilian ones were some distance away from towns. There are exceptions in small clusters near Colchester, London, and Verulamium, and in a series of as yet not fully excavated kilns at Minety, which almost certainly supplied brick for Cirencester – at one time the second largest town in Roman Britain.

The recent increase of investigation into the fabric of brick and tile has been valuable, but we need to discover many more kilns with more excavation of the areas around them. In the past pottery has had ample attention, while the less glamorous brick, which is economically much more important, has been neglected. There are only a handful of sites whose tile can be linked with certainty to a particular kiln. It is only when some special feature such as a stamp or some roller-patterned imprint is present that it is possible to plot connection between finds. McWhirr and Viner (1978) have made a special study of stamped tile in the Cotswold area, and the present writer has studied the stamped tiles of the *Classis Britannica* (Brodribb, 1969 and 1980). At Beauport Park in East Sussex over 1600 complete or partial examples of CL BR stamps have been found – all from a small bath-house. A hundred years ago there was a brickworks in the same area and it was thought that possibly the same local clay had once been used to make the Roman tile. Fabric tests by Mike Stone have shown however that the CL BR tiles were of quite different fabric from that of the more recent products. So the Roman tile must have been brought in from elsewhere – a problem of transport in such a desolate and wooded area. It is increasingly thought that heavy goods such as tile were taken not so much by road as by small waterways no longer navigable but perfectly adequate in Roman times.

The CL BR tiles were probably made at some official fleet depot.

This kiln site has yet to be discovered or may have unfortunately vanished into the sea. Evidence for a central depot is supported by a particular flaw in one type of die which appears on the majority of fleet sites. Another valuable fact proved by fabric investigation is that three of the CL BR sites – Dover, Lympne and Beauport Park – all possess some tiles which have a fabric that came from France, while at Boulogne there are stamps which were produced in Britain (Peacock, 1977). When we have more details like these, we will eventually learn more about the distribution of brick and tile.

It is very difficult to give any exact dating for much of the tile and brick surveyed here. Even if a building can be given some firm date, there is no guarantee that the tile used for it was new at the time. So often a report speaks of tile 'found in infill for a new floor' or 'box-tiles from an earlier bath now used as a drain'. This all suggests a great deal of alteration and consquent re-use of tile even in Roman times. The wider the range of time spanned by a building the more likely re-use becomes, and in post-Roman times there are many examples of Roman material used in the building of churches.

There are however a number of firm dating points. Some legionary fortresses can provide evidence, e.g. the forts at Exeter and Usk have tile known to be as early as AD 60–65; tile found beneath the levels of Boudiccan destruction at Colchester must be earlier than AD 61; the uncompleted bath at Inchtuthil dates to about AD 83–87; there are fine examples of legionary buildings at Gelligaer (c. AD 103–112) and Housesteads (c. AD 124–6); the *Classis Britannica* stamped tile, at least at Beauport Park, dated from c. AD 120, which means that CL BR tile found at Lympne and Dover (Saxon Shore fort), which have rebuilding dates of c. AD 280, could be reused tile from earlier times. Though it must be accepted that for much of the material no exact date is possible, it would be reasonable to suggest that the manufacture of new tile must have increased with times of Roman expansion, and dwindled both in quantity and quality towards the end of the Occupation. Vitruvius himself recommended the use of old tile, and the practice of re-using time-tested material is still maintained.

APPENDIX I *ANALYSIS OF ITEMS IN THE SURVEY*

Number of Sites	Type of Tile or Brick	Items			Average measurements (mm)		
		Complete	Partial	Total	Long	Wide	Deep
212	Tegula	615	395	1010	430	330	50 (ext fl)
127	Imbrex	320	111	431	398	177–137	91 (tall)
22	Ridge tile	8	24	32	377	234	133 (tall)
133	Bessalis	1132	6	1138	198		43
22	Bessalis (round)	76	1	77	219 (diam)		42
71	Pedalis	201	2	203	281		46
109	Lydion	314	73	387	403	280	41
26	Sesquipedalis	42	10	52	406		52
33	Bipedalis	23	24	47	577		60
27	Cuneatus	62	14	76	382	292	63–42
				or	372	146	
13	Cuneatus 'Armchair'	7	9	16	358	355	54
15	Semi-circular	22	6	28	338		56
19	Quadrant	24	6	30	188		54
13	Oblong	16	11	27	381	140	47
30	Opus spicatum	574	0	574	114	62	26

Number of Sites	Type of Tile or Brick	Items			Average measurements (mm)		
		Complete	Partial	Total	Long	Wide	Deep
18	Parietalis	5	25	30	402	270	28
24	Half-box	16	26	42	453	337	79 (ext fl)
166	Box-tile	306	340	646	366	190	131
13	Double-box	16	31	47	345	301	160
70	Voussoir	71	110	181	255	173–144	137
11	'Springers'	24	3	27	230	195–166	121
18	Spacer bobbins	70	52	122	80	57 (diam)	
40	Pipes	123	42	165	371	129 (ext diam)	
73	Unclassified	0	309	309			
60	Unidentified	42	62	104			
23	? Kiln	26	24	50			
		4135	1716	5851			

1   Percentages of features of various types of brick

Type	Signature	Stamp	Print	Tally-mark	Graffito	Mamma
Bessalis	14.3	8.3	4.6	2.4	1.3	0.8
Bessalis (round)	2.7	2.7				
Pedalis	23.0	8.5	4.0	1.0	2.0	1.0
Lydion	25.7	2.5	7.3		2.0	15.0
Sesquipedalis	42.8	14.2	9.5	0.7		21.4
Bipedalis	39.1	17.3	0.8	0.8		30.4
Cuneatus	22.3	7.4		0.1		
Semi-circular	9.0	13.6				
Quadrant		4.1				
Oblong	6.2		12.5			
Total	19.0	7.4	5.0	1.7	1.3	4.0

2 Roofing and other signed tile

Type	Signature	Stamp	Print	Tally-mark	Graffito	Nail hole	No Groove	Double Groove	Cut-Out
Tegula	61.0	12.0	4.5	3.4	1.0	19.3	4.9	2.5	90 (1, 5) 10 (2, 3, 4)
Imbrex & RT	14.1	19.9							
Parietalis	80.0 (scoring)	60.0	1.6	0.3		80.0			
Half-box	26.0	20.0							

3 Flue tile

Type	Vent	Stamp	Graffito	Round corners
Tubulus	70.6			
Double-box	87.0	2.1	1.4	3.2
Voussoir	41.0			
Total	66.0			

APPENDIX II *HIGH-STANDING ROMAN WALLS*

High-standing Roman walls, even when made of material other than brick, are extremely rare in Britain. Apart from considerable structures such as the walls of forts, e.g. at Pevensey (28 feet or 8.5m), Richborough (25 feet or 7.6m), Portchester (25 feet or 7.6m), and some town walls, e.g. at London (14 feet 6 inches or 4.4m), Chester (17 feet or 5.1m), and York (15 feet or 4.5m), other remains seldom stand to any great height. Time, weather, and spoliation have played havoc with them, and even the walls of forts and towns have often had their facing nibbled away by predators. This robbing of building material was not solely a post-Roman practice, for it had developed widely in the later period of Roman Britain. There is considerable evidence of robbing of the never-completed early baths at Wroxeter, and how the robbers dug very deep and dangerously even down to footings and drains in their search for brick that could be gainfully used. (Pers. comm. Graham Webster)

But there are a few rare survivors, and one of two obvious examples of high-standing building is the 'Old Work' at Wroxeter, which was originally part of the south wall of a large aisled building. It extends for 70 feet (21.3m), is 3 feet (910mm) thick, and stands 20 feet (6.1m) high (probably the original height of Hadrian's Wall). Situated in open fields the 'Old Work' is impressive, and it is a miracle that it has stood so well while the rest of the building vanished.

The other example is the 'Jewry Wall' at Leicester which stands as much as 35 feet (10.6m). It formed part of the west wall of the exercise hall and public baths, and it has survived chiefly because it may have been incorporated into the nearby church.

Among much smaller buildings, the military bath-house at Ravenglass (known as 'Walls Castle') has remains that stand to 12 feet 6 inches (3.81m) high. It is a building on level ground in a wood next to a public way, and its survival seems almost uncanny. Traces of five windows can be seen with sills 4 feet (1.22m) from ground-floor levels. Roman buildings in Britain rarely stand high enough to show evidence of windows, and the only comparable windows are at Chesters bath-house where the sill of a window over the apse of the hot bath is as much as 6 feet above the floor, and at Beauport Park where the windows in Room 3 have a sill standing 4 feet 2 inches (1.27m) with side pieces rising on each side. There are also signs of a window at Great Chesters (Aesica), while at Colliton Park, Dorchester, a crashed piece of wall, now replaced, gives evidence of a window with a sill 30 inches (760mm) from ground level, rising to 4 feet 2 inches (1.27m) at the top of the uprights.

The only other evidence of windows in Romano-British buildings is found in cellars below ground level, where they had a much better chance of survival.

The Balkerne Gate, Colchester, is one of the best monuments in Roman Britain. It consists of two carriageways 5.5m wide, and two footways 2m wide, flanked by D-shaped bastions, one of which stands to as much as 6.6m (19 feet) high. Built into this gate is an old inn 'The Hole in the Wall', and this is the reason for the survival of the whole structure. Another notable gateway is the north gate at Lincoln, known as the Newport Arch and it is the only Roman gateway in Britain through which traffic still passes.

Another Roman structure, though repaired by the Normans is the Pharos on the Castle Hill at Dover. This light-house is an octagonal tower, and the walls are 10 feet (3m) thick making an internal area of 14 feet (4.2m) square. The present height is about 40 feet (12m) and the lower levels are original first century AD work. The Mint wall at Lincoln, west of Bailgate, runs for a distance of 22.5m and stands up to 7.25m (23.7 feet) high. Triple tile courses occur at intervals of *c.* 1.6m.

Other high-standing walls belonging to individual small buildings are very rare unless they were fortuitously buried in the slope of a hill. These include the bath-house at Chesters (already mentioned), the rooms of the Painted House at Dover, and the bath-house at the Roman ironworks at Beauport Park. Here the walls stand up to 8 feet (2.4m) high, and it is estimated that at least 60 per cent of the walls are still standing.

APPENDIX III
FORMATIONS OF *TEGULA MAMMATA*

Sites which have complete examples or evidence to show a formation are listed here, and the type of brick is also indicated e.g. B : bessalis,   P : pedalis,   L : lydion,   S : sesquipedalis,   and Bip : bipedalis.

Group A (Single *mamma* set centrally)

Wiggonholt (B & P)	Gelligaer (B)	Braughing (P)
Colchester (L)	London (L)	Silchester (L)
Fishbourne (L)	Chichester (B)	Verulamium (L)
Staines (L)		

Group B (Single *mamma* set in one corner)

Canterbury (L)

Group C (Two *mammae* set diagonally at opposite corners)

Hardham (L)	Fishbourne (L)	Chanctonbury Ring (L)
Southwick (L)	Pulborough (L)	Alfoldean Bridge (L)
Winchester (L)	Chichester (L)	London (L & S)
Angmering (L)		Alfoldean Gate (L)

Group D (Two *mammae* set adjacent at one end)

Angmering (L)	Fishbourne (L)	Dorchester, Dorset (L)

Group E (Two *mammae* set adjacent but centrally)

Gelligaer (S)

Group F (Three *mammae* set in a triangular position)

Holcombe

Group G (Four *mammae*, one set at each corner)

Braughing (U)	Dorchester, Dorset (L)	Alfoldean Bridge (L)
London (S & Bip)	Bodiam (Bip)	Beauport Park (S & Bip)
Chichester (Bip)	Dover (Bip)	Richborough (Bip)
Gelligaer (Bip)	Folkestone (Bip)	Highdown (P)

Group H (Four *mammae* set centred in middle of each side)

Lincoln (S)

Also given here is a list of other sites whose examples are labelled 'Unclassified' because with only one *mamma* visible there is no evidence of the formation of *mammae* or type of brick.

Ashstead	Cranbrook	Maidstone
Bardown	Cricklade	Minety
Bodiam	Dorchester (Dorset)	Mucking
Boulogne	Eccles	Plumpton
Brading	Elsted	Pulborough
Braughing	Fishbourne	Richborough
Canterbury	Fishbourne Harbour	Seaford
Chanctonbury Ring	Folkestone	Silchester
Chelmsford	Gorhambury	Stonea
Chichester	Havant	Wiggonholt
Chignall St James	Lancaster	Winchester
Chitcombe	London	Wroxeter
Clausentum		

APPENDIX IV   BOX-TILE FEATURES

Percentages of the variety of surface treatment of box-tile and hollow voussoir, based upon the 253 complete listed examples.

Type	Examples	Combed	Scored	Roller-printed	Left plain
Box-tile	195	90	69	26	10
Double-box	6	0	3	3	0
Voussoir	52	31	9	2	10
Total	253	121	81	31	20
Percentage		47.8	32	12.2	7.9

The predominance of combing is further evident when note is made of what type of treatment each site produced rather than the total of examples.

Type	Sites	Combed	Scored	Roller-printed	Left plain
Box-tile	78	49	18	9	4
Double-box	5	0	3	3	0
Voussoir	23	15	2	2	1
Total	106	64	23	14	5
Percentage		60.3	21.6	13.2	4.6

GLOSSARY

NB. Terms underlined are classical words

ACROTERIA   Projecting parts of a pediment serving as support for figures.

ANTEFIX   A moulded object of clay sometimes slotted into the end of the lowest course of *imbrex* on a roof or set at the end of the ridge. It often carried some emblem.

APODYTERIUM   The dressing room or 'leisure centre' of a bath-house.

BESSALIS   A flat square brick of about 8 inches (200 mm) used most commonly to form a *pila* in a hypocaust.

BIPEDALIS   A flat square brick measuring 2 ft (580 mm).

BOBBIN SPACER   A rare form of cavity heating was created by flat wall tile being separated from the inner wall by means of reel-like clay bobbins held in place by long cramps or holdfasts running through the middle.

BONDING COURSE   In a wall made of masonry or flint a course of brick is laid at certain intervals which helps to bond the whole section together before a new level of wall is raised.

BOX-FLUE TILE (or BOX-TILE)   A hollow tile (about the size of an open-ended shoe-box) set to act as a flue to carry hot air : it is in fact a square pipe built up in sections.

BRICK   The joint term 'Brick and Tile' covers most forms of ceramic building material : for some 'Tile' is a more proper term, e.g. roof-tile, and box-tile, while for others, such as flat forms of all sizes, 'Brick' is the more usual term.

CALDARIUM   The hot room in a bath-house.

CAPPING   At the top of each *pila* a larger brick is placed as a cap, and above this even larger ones are set to form the basis of a floor.

CHAMFERED   Sometimes an edge of a tile or the flange of a *tegula* is cut off in a slope or bevel.

'CHIMNEY-POT'   A ceramic object shaped like a tower or *pharos* with a series of portions cut out : set on a roof to allow smoke or fumes to escape. There may be other uses.

CIST   Hollowed out container for burial purposes.

CLASSIS BRITANNICA   The Romano-British Fleet apart from its naval and transport duties was also in charge of the Iron Industry in the S.E.

150

of Britain. Tiles used in buildings concerned with the fleet often carry the fleet stamp – usually the letters CL BR.

COMB   A comb made of wood or bone made even parallel lines on the face of tile that was to be covered with plaster, and this combing helped the plaster to be keyed on.

CORNICE   A moulded projection crowning the wall of a building.

COVING   Quarter-round plaster moulding set at the join of wall and floor to make it easier for cleaning or washing.

CRAMP   A metal object such as a T-headed long nail used for holding tile such as box-flue tile in position. Also known as 'holdfast'.

'CUT-AWAY'   A portion of tile deliberately cut-away before baking, e.g. the portion of the lower end of the flange on a *tegula*. The purpose is usually to assist the fitting together with adjacent tile.

'CUT-OUT'   A portion of tile cut out of a surface e.g. those cut out of the sides of box-flue tiles to allow hot-air to circulate laterally or to provide a vent to allow fumes to escape.

DIE   An object made of wood, clay or metal in which lettering has been engraved so as to produce a stamp when the die is impressed upon the tile. For the stamp to come out correctly the letters have to be cut retrograde.

DOUBLE-BOX   Some large box-flue tiles are divided down the middle to form two boxes within one tile.

FABRIC   The body of the clay used to make ceramic objects. There are many varieties of clay, and different fabrics can be identified.

FINIAL   An ornament for finishing off the apex of a roof.

FOOTING   A solid often projecting foundation course made of large slabs of stone or tile on which the wall is mounted.

FRIGIDARIUM   The cold room of a bath-house containing a cold plunge.

'HALF BOX'   As these resemble large box-flue tiles cut down the middle they are known as a 'half-boxes'.

HERRINGBONE FLOOR   A floor surface composed of small bricks laid in a herringbone pattern, cf. a modern parquet-floor.

HOLDFAST   See CRAMP.

HYPOCAUST   The area below a floor suspended on *pilae* in which hot air from the adjacent furnace (*praefurnium*) can circulate, and then make its way up the walls by means of flues.

IMBREX   A tile of semi-circular shape used mostly to cover over the flanges of two adjacent *tegulae*.

IMPRESSION   The visible signs of some object being impressed upon a soft clay surface. It ranges from an official stamp to that of a coin, buckle or leaf.

KILN-FURNITURE   A general term for ceramic items mainly concerned with stacking of a kiln, e.g. props, supports, pads etc.

LACONIAN   A method of roofing in which *imbrices* only are used, set over-and-under throughout.

LACONICUM   A very hot dry sweating room in a bath-house.

LATER   A general name for any clay brick that has been baked.

LYDION   A flat brick that measures on average 400 × 280 mm, often found in bonding courses.

MOSAIC   The design in which *tesserae* are laid on a floor surface.

OPUS SECTILE   A decorative form of flooring made up of various specially-cut shapes of marble, clay etc.

OPUS SPICATUM   See Herringbone floor.

PARIETALIS   The Latin for wall is *paries*, and *parietalis* tile is that fixed vertically to a wall, held in position by cramps.

PAVIMENTUM   A hard floor composed of small stones and earth beaten down.

PEDALIS   A square flat brick measuring 1 ft (280 mm).

PILAE   The pillars or piers mounted on the floor of the hypocaust to hold up the floor above (*suspensura*): usually formed of *bessalis* brick.

PRAEFURNIUM   Next to the hypocaust is the furnace in which wood fuel is burnt to provide hot air to be drawn into the hypocaust.

PUT-LOG HOLES   Holes made in the masonry of a wall into which beams were slotted to hold up scaffolding.

QUADRANT   One of the four parts when a circular tile is cut into four. Two of these could be used to create half-columns.

RELIEF   A method of stamping in which the design or lettering stands out raised from the surface. This is the opposite to stamping in which the lettering is indented into the surface.

RETROGRADE   The die for a tile-stamp has to be cut in reverse in order to come out the right way, (cf. the positive and negative of a photograph). If the die is copied directly from the stamp it will, when impressed, come out in reverse or retrograde.

RIDGE-TILE   The ridge on a roof where the *tegulae* meet on each side is covered by a curved tile, often an ordinary *imbrex*, but sometimes by a specially made ridge-tile of similar shape but larger.

ROLLER PRINTING   Tile which is to be covered with plaster is either combed or scored, or alternatively marked with lines or patterns put on by a special roller by which the area is covered more quickly.

SCORING   In order to make a key for plaster to be imposed on tile, the surface of the tile may be scored over, often in a lattice pattern, with a knife point or sharp instrument.

SEGMENTED BRICK   Brick of geometrical shape used to form columns or half-columns.

SESQUIPEDALIS   A square flat brick measuring 2 ft (410 mm).

SHINGLES   Some roofs are covered with small flat rectangular pieces of wood (usually oak), laid like tiles.

SIGNATURE   Lines, often of a semi-circular pattern, are often seen marked on the face of tile, usually imposed with the finger. The diversity of such markings suggests the personal effort of some particular tile-maker, hence the word 'signature'.

'SPRINGER'   Hollow tile similar to voussoir but different in that one side is a right angle, while the other has a slope. Such tile makes a suitable starting piece from which an arch made of voussoirs can spring.

STAMP   Some official bodies stamped their tile as proof of ownership e.g. the Legions and the Fleet. A very wide range of stamp can be found.

SUDATORUM   A room in a bath-house which provides special opportunities for sweating.

SUSPENSURA   The floor that lies above a hypocaust usually suspended on *pilae*.

TALLY-MARK   Some tile carries marks cut on the edge that resemble Roman numerals: these may signify the recording of various batches of production.

TEGULA   A flat roof tile with a raised flange each side : the adjacent flanges are then covered with an *imbrex*.

TEGULA MAMMATA   Flat tile with lumps of clay (mamma : breast) superimposed either to act as a key to prevent slipping when the tiles are used in a bonding course, or, with a deeper pointed variety, to form a spacer when the tile is mounted vertically to provide cavity heating space.

TEPIDARIUM   The slightly warm room in a bath-house.

TESSELATED   A floor surface composed of *tesserae*.

TESSERAE   Small specially cut cubes of stone or tile used to form a tesselated floor in mosaic pattern.

TILE   See BRICK.

TILE TOMB   A burial covering made up of a series of *tegulae* and *imbrices* built in the form of a hut with a sloping roof.

TRACK   The mark of the series of parallel lines left after a comb has been used on a tile.

TUBULATIO   The whole system of heating rooms both underfloor and up the walls by means of hot air carried by box-flue tiles.

TUBULATUS CUNEATUS   See VOUSSOIR.

TUFA   A rock form sometimes used for building : its extreme lightness makes it suitable for arches. It is volcanic in origin.

VOUSSOIR   A hollow or solid tile with taper on two edges generally used to form arches. The hollow variety enables hot air to circulate or help to lighten the weight of the structure.

BIBLIOGRAPHY

The following abbreviations have been used both in the text and in the bibliography. They conform to the CBA standard list of titling.

Antiq J	:	Antiquaries Journal
Archaeologia	:	Archaeologia
Archaeol Aeliana	:	Archaeologia Aeliana
Archaeol Cambrensis	:	Archaeologia Cambrensis
Archaeol Cantiana	:	Archaeologia Cantiana
Archaeol J	:	Archaeological Journal
Britannia	:	Britannia
Brit Archaeol Rep	:	British Archaeological Reports
J Brit Archaeol Ass	:	Journal of the British Archaeological Association
J Roman Stud	:	Journal of Roman Studies
Surrey Archaeol Collect	:	Surrey Archaeological Collections
Sussex Archaeol Collect	:	Sussex Archaeological Collections
CBA	:	Council for British Archaeology
CIL	:	Corpus Inscriptorum Latinorum
EE	:	Ephemeris Epigraphica
VCH	:	Victoria County History

Bibliography of Classical Authors

(The English form of title has been used where it seems suitable)

D. Magnus AUSONIUS	Parentalia
M. Porcius CATO	De Agri Cultura
L. Iulius Moderatus COLUMELLA	De Re Rustica
DIOCLETIAN	Edict (ed. Erim and Reynolds)
DIO CASSIUS	History of Rome
ISODORUS HISPALENSIS	Origines
T. LIVIUS Patavinus	History of Rome (Ab Urbe Condita)

PALLADIUS Rutilius Taurus	Opus Agriculturae
T. Maccius PLAUTUS	Comedies
C. PLINIUS Secundus	Naturalis Historia
C. PLINIUS Caecilius Secundus (the Younger)	Letters
PLUTARCHUS	Parallel Lives
L. Annaeus SENECA (the Younger)	De Providentia, Epistulae Morales, Naturales Quaestiones
G. Lollius SIDONIUS APOLLINARIS	Epistulae
Aelius SPARTIANUS	Scriptores Historiae Augustae
P. Papinius STATIUS	Silvae
C. SUETONIUS Tranquillus	De Vita Caesarum (Augustus & Nero)
P. TERENTIUS Afer	Phormio
Domitius ULPIANUS	Corpus Iuris Civilis
VALERIUS MAXIMUS	Facta ac Dicta Memorabilia
P. VIRGILIUS Maro	Aeneid, Georgics
L. VITRUVIUS Pollio	De Architectura

General Bibliography

The following authors are referred to in the text. Apart from these a Select Bibliography follows which is entirely concerned with items connected with Stamped Tile.

Acton, F.S. 1846	'A Roman villa discovered at Acton Scott, Shropshire', Archaeologia 31 (1846)
Amos, E.G.J. 1921	Note in J Roman Stud 11 (1921), 239, 13
Artis, E.T. 1828	The Durobrivae of Antoninus, London, 1828
Bell, R.C. 1960	Board and Table Games, London, 1960
Bertram, R.J.S. 1931	Illustration in G. Macdonald's 'The Bath-house at the Fort of Chesters', Archaeol Aeliana (4 ser) 8, 1931
Bidwell, P.T. 1979	'The Legionary Bath-house and Basilica and Forum at Exeter', Exeter Archaeol Report I, Exeter 1979
Black, E.W. 1985a	'Hypocaust Heating in Domestic Rooms' in Oxford J. of Arch. Vol 4, I, 1985
Black, E.W. 1985b	'The dating of relief-patterned flue-tiles' in Oxford J. of Arch, vol 4, 3 1985

Blagg, T.F.C. 1979 — 'The use of terra-cotta for architectural ornament in Italy and the Western Provinces', Brit Archaeol Rep 68 (1979), 267–84

Blake, M.E. 1947 — Ancient Rome construction in Italy from the prehistoric period to Augustus', Washington, 1947

Blake, M.E. 1959 — Roman construction from Tiberius through the Flavians, Washington, 1959

Blake, M.E. and Bishop, D.T. 1973 — Roman construction in Italy from Nerva through the Antonines, edited and completed by D.T. Bishop, Philadelphia, 1973.

Blumlein, H. 1926 — Bilder aus dem Romisch-Germanisch kulturben, Munich, 1926

Boon, G.C. 1974 — Silchester, the Roman town of Calleva, Newton Abbot, 1974 edition

Boon, G.C. 1980 — The Brick and Tile stamps of the second Augustan Legion, privately issued, 1980

Boon, G.C. 1984 — Laterarium Iscanum, Cardiff, 1984

Brodribb, A.G.C., Hands, A.R. & Walker, D.R. — Excavations at Shakenoak Farm, near Wilcote, Oxfordshire, Vol iv, Oxford, 1973

Brodribb, G. 1973 — Note in Britannia 4 (1973), 333

Brodribb, G. 1979 — 'Tile from the bath-house at Beauport Park', (Britannia 10, 1979, 139–156)

Brogan, O. 1953 — Roman Gaul, London, 1953

Bruce, J. Collingwood 1863 — Wallet of the Wall, Newcastle, 1863

Budge, E.A. 1907 — An account of Roman antiquities preserved at Chesters, 2nd ed. 1907, items 629–49

Cazzare, F. 1976 — Deux tombes sous tegulae à Ollieres, Centre de coordination et de documentation archaeologique de Provence, Cahier no. 4, Fev. 1976

Chauffin, J. 1956 — 'Tuiles du Bas-Dauphiné', Gallia 14 (1956)

Corder, P. & Kirk, J.L. 1932 — 'A Roman villa at Langton, nr Malton, E. Yorks.' Roman Malton & District Report 4, Leeds, 1932

Cram, L. & Fulford, M.G. 1979 — 'Silchester tile-making – the Faunal Environment' in 'Roman Brick and Tile' (ed. A. McWhirr), Brit Archaeol Rep 68 (1979) 201–09

Cuming, S.H. 1869 — 'A few words on forgeries', J Brit Archaeol Ass 25 (1869)

Cunliffe, B.W. 1969 — Roman Bath (Soc. Ant. Report XXIV), Oxford, 1969

Cunliffe, B.W. 1971 — Excavations at Fishbourne (Soc. Ant. Report XXVI) vol. ii, Oxford, 1971

Daniels, C.M. 1959 — 'The Roman Bath-house at Red House', Archaeol Aeliana 37 (4 ser) (1959), 170

Davey, N. 1945 — 'The Roman villa at Park St. At Albans' Archaeol J 102 (1945), 106

Davey, N. 1961 — A History of Building Materials, London, 1961

Davies, G. 1857 — 'Roman remains at Caersws', Archaeol Cambrensis 3 (1857)

de Pachtere, F.G. 1912 — Paris, l'epoque Gallo-Romaine, Paris, 1912

Dessau, H. 1882 — Inscriptiones Latinae Selectae, Berlin, 1882

Diamond, S.A. 1975 — 'The Historical development of Trade marks', The Trade mark Reporter 65 (1975)

Dobson, C.G. 1960 — Historical notes on the Langley Museum, London, 1960

Dunning, G.C. & Corder, P. 1943 — Note in J Roman Stud 33 (1943), 80–111

Elford, A. 1941 — Note in American J of Archaeology, 45 (1941)

Erim, K.T. & Reynolds, J. 1973 — 'The Aphrodisias copy of Diocletian's Edict on Maximum Prices', J Roman Stud 63 (1973)

Fennelly, L.R. 1969 — 'Excavation of the Roman villa at Combley, Arreton, I.W. 1968–9', Proc Isle Wight Hist Antiq Soc 6 (part iv) 1969

Forster, R.H. & Knowles, W.H. 1910 — Report on the Excavations at Corstopitum (Reprints from Archaeol Aeliana, 3 (ser vi & vii) 1910, 1911)

Fox, N.P. 1955 — 'Warbank, Keston : a Romano-British site', Archaeol Cantiana 69 (1955)

Gautier, G. 1902 — 'Les Bains de la villa Gallo-Romaine de Champvert, Nicvrc', Bull Arch Comite des Traveaux Historiques et Scientifiques, 1902

Gentry, A.P. 1976 — 'Roman military stone-built granaries in Britain', Brit Archaeol Rep 32 (1976)

Gillam, J.P. 1978 — Note in Antiq J 58-2 (1978), 389

Gilyard-Beer, R. 1951 — The Romano-British Baths at Wall (Yorkshire Archaeol Research Report No. I), Leeds, 1951

Giraldus Cambrensis c.1188 — The Journey through Wales (1188), Book II, ch.5

Goodchild, R.G. 1937 — 'The Roman Brickworks at Wykehurst Farm', Surrey Archaeol Collect 45 (1937)

Gough, R. 1786 — Sepulchral Monuments, vol. ii, London, 1786, xxiii

Graham, A. 1886 — 'Remains of Roman occupation of North

Africa, Trans Royal Institute of British Archi-tects, I (N ser), (1886)

Green, H.J.M. 1959 An Architectural Survey of the Roman Baths at Godmanchester, The Archaeological Newsletter 6 (1959)

Green, T.K. 1970 'Roman Tileworks at Ichingfield', Sussex Archaeol Collect 108 (1970)

Green, T.K. 1979 'Techniques for studying comb signature dis-tributions', Brit Archaeol Rep 68 (1979), 364

Greenaway, J. 1981 'The Neronian stamped tile from Little London, near Silchester; Britannia 12 (1981)

Grimes, W.F. 1930 'Holt, Denbighshire, the works depot of the Twentieth Legion at Castle Lyons, Y Cym-mrodor 41 (1930)

Gunther, R.T. 1913 Pausilypon, Oxford, 1913

Hanworth, R. 1968 'The Roman villa at Rapsley, Ewhurst', Surrey Archaeol Collect 65 (1968)

Hawkes, C.F.C. & Hull, M.R. 1947 Camulodumum (Soc. Ant. Report XIV), Oxford, 1947

Hodder, I. 1974 a 'The distribution of two types of Romano-British coarse pottery in the West Sussex region', Sussex Archaeol Collect 112 (1974)

Hodder, I. 1974 b 'Some market models for coarse pottery', Britannia 5 (1974), 340 etc.

Hofmann, B. 1975 'Les materieux de construction antique en terre cuite', Les Dossiers de l'archaeologie ceramique en Gaule Romaine, No. 9, Mars-Avril, 1975

Hoopell, R.E. 1891 Vinovia, a buried Roman city, London, 1891

Hope, W.H.St J. & Fox, G.E. 1901 'Excavations on the site of the Roman city at Silchester, Hants. in 1900, Archaeologia 57 (1901)

Hope, W.H.St J. 1907 'Excavations on the site of the Roman city of Silchester, Hants. in 1906', Archaeologia 60 (1907)

Hopkinson, J.H. 1906 'The Pottery' in Melandra Castle (ed. R.S. Conway), Manchester, 1906

Hull, M.R. 1958 Roman Colchester (Soc. Ant. Report XX), Oxford, 1958

Hultsch, F. 1882 Griechische und Romishe Metrologie (1882), Graz, 1971 edition, 700

Jahn, V. 1909 'Die Romischen Dachziegel von Windisch', Anzeiger fur Schweizerische Alterumsckunde 11 (1909)

Jenkins, F. 1956 'A Roman tilery and two pottery kilns at

Durovernum (Canterbury)', Antiq J 36 (1956)

Johnstone, D.E. & Williams, D.F. 1979 — 'Relief-patterned tiles – a reappraisal', Brit Archaeol Rep 68 (1979)

Jones, M.U. 1972 — 'Potters' graffiti from Mucking, Essex', Antiq J 52 (1972)

Jones, M.U. 1981 — Note on tegula moulded stamps from Stanton Low, Antiq J 61–2, 1981

Kenyon, K.M. 1940 — 'Excavations at Viroconium', Archaeologia 88 (1940)

Lanciani, R. 1897 — The Ruins and excavations of ancient Rome, Boston and New York, 1897, 39

Laver, H. 1907 — 'On a Roman villa recently discovered at Grimston, Norfolk', Norfolk Archaeol 16 (1907)

Lee, J.E. 1862 — Isca Silurum, London, 1862

Leighton, 1789 — Memoir on a Roman bath discovered at Wroxeter in 1788', Archaeologia 9 (1789)

Lethaby, W.R. 1923 — Londonium : architecture and the crafts, London, 1923

Lowther, A.W.G. 1927 — 'Excavations at Ashstead', Surrey Archaeol Collect 37 (1927)

Lowther, A.W.G. 1930 — 'Excavations at Ashstead', Surrey Archaeol Collect 38 (1930)

Lowther, A.W.G. 1937 — Excavations at Verulam, Antiq J 17 (1937)

Lowther, A.W.G. 1945 — 'Relief patterned flue tiles in the Roman villa at Park St., St Albans', Archaeol J 102 (1945)

Lowther, A.W.G. 1948 — 'A study of patterns on Roman flue-tiles and their distribution', Research Paper I of Surrey Archaeol Soc, 1948

Lowther, A.W.G. 1976 — 'Romano-British chimney pots and finials' (ed. F.H. Thomson), Antiq J 56–1 (1976), 35–48

Ludovici, W. 1912 — Ausgrabungen in Rheinabern, vol. iv, 1912

Lugli, G. 1957 — La Technica Edilizia Romana, Rome, 1957

Lyon, J. 1779 — 'Description of a Roman bath discovered at Dover', Archaeologia 5 (1779)

Lyon, J. 1813 — History of the town and port of Dover, vol. I, Dover, 1813

Lysons, S. 1797 — Roman Antiquities at Woodchester, London, 1797

Lysons, S. 1817 — 'An account of several Roman buildings and other Roman antiquities discovered in the county of Gloucester', Archaeologia 18 (1817)

Lysons, S. 1821 — 'An account of a Roman villa discovered at Great Witcombe', Archaeologia 19 (1821)

McCann, J. 1982 — 'Reading the Timber : part 5, Carpenter's Marks', Period Home, vol 2, no 4, Dec-Jan 1982

McWhirr, A.D. 1979 — Editor 'Roman Brick and Tile', Brit Archaeol Rep 68 (1979)

McWhirr, A.D. 1979 — 'Tile kilns in Roman Britain', Brit Archaeol Rep 68 (1979)

McWhirr, A.D. & Viner, D. 1978 — 'Production and distribution of Tiles', Britannia 9 (1978)

Manning, W.H. & Webster, P.V. 1978 — 'Romano-British Tile from Usk, Gwent', Antiq J 58–2 (1978)

Maiuri, A. 1931 — 'La villa dei Misteri', Rome, 1931

May, T. 1922 — The Roman Forts at Templebrough, Rothererham, 1922

Meates, G.W. 1955 — Lullingstone Roman Villa, London, 1955

Merrifield, R. 1969 — Roman London, London, 1969

Middleton, J.H. 1892 — Remains of Ancient Rome, London, 1892

Money, J.H. 1974 — 'Clay spacers from the Romano-British Bath-house at Garden Hill, Hartfield; Antiq J 54 (1974)

Moray Williams, A. 1909 — 'A Roman British establishment at Stroud, nr Petersfield, Hants', Archaeol J 47 (1909)

Morgan, G. 1979 — 'Experiments in making and firing box flue tiles', Brit Archaeol Rep 68 (1979)

Morley-Hewitt, A.T. 1968 — The Roman villa at West Park, Rockbourne, 2nd ed 1968

Myers, J.N.L. 1969 — Anglo-Saxon pottery and the settlements of England, Oxford, 1969

Nash-Williams, V.E. 1969 — The Roman Frontier in Wales, Univ. Wales, Cardiff 2nd ed. 1969 (revised by M.G. Jarrett)

Neal, D.S. 1974 — The Excavation of the Roman villa at Gadebridge Park, Hemel Hempstead, (Soc Ant Report xxxi) London, 1974

Neal, D.S. 1976 — 'Northchurch, Boxmoor, and Hemel Hempstead Station: the excavation of three Roman buildings in the Bulborne Valley', 1976 (Reprint from Hertfordshire Archaeol 4, 1976)

Newstead, R. & Droop, J.P. 1936 — 'Excavations in the Deanery Field and Abbey Green, 1935', Liverpool Annals and Archaeology 23 (1936)

Orsi, P. 1914 — 'Caulonia', Monumenti Antichi 23 (1914)

Payne, G. 1897   'A Roman villa at Darenth', Archaeol Cantiana 22 (1897)

Peacock, D.P.S. 1979   'An Ethnoarchaeological approach to the study of Roman Bricks', Brit Archaeol Rep 68 (1979)

Philp, B.J. 1971   Note in Britannia 2 (1971)

Piranesi, G.B. 1748   Antichita Romana, vol. iii, Rome, 1748

Pollard, S., 1974   A late Iron-age settlement and a Romano-British villa at Holcombe, near Uplyme, Devon, Torquay, 1974 (Reprint Proc Devon Archaeol Soc 32 (1974))

Popilian, G. 1971   'Thermele de la Slaveni', Apulum 9 (1971)

Price, Hilton, F.G. 1887   'Further notes on excavation at Silchester' Archaeologia 50 (1887)

Richmond, I.A. 1966   Note in Sussex Archaeol Collect 104 (1966)

Rivoira, G.T. 1925   The Architecture of Ancient Rome, Oxford, 1925

Roach Smith, C. 1845   'Roman London', Archaeol J I (1845)

Roach Smith, C. 1849   'Notes on a Roman building discovered in Lower Thames St., in the city of London', J Brit Archaeol Ass 4 (1849)

Roach Smith, C. 1859   Illustrations of Roman London, iii, London, 1859

Rook, A.G. 1979   'Tiled Roofs', Brit Archaeol Rep 68 (1979)

Rudder, S. 1779   A new history of Gloucestershire, Cirencester, 1779

Scarth, H.M. 1864   Aquae Sulis or Notices of Roman Bath, Bath, 1864

Scott, K. 1971   'Two Romano-British tile kilns', Trans Birmingham Warwickshire Archaeol Soc 84 (1971)

Scott, L. 1938   'The Roman villa at Angmering', Sussex Archaeol Collect 79 (1938)

Stephenson, M. 1915   'A Roman Building found at Compton', Surrey Archaeol Collect 28 (1915)

Stone, P.G. 1929   'A Roman villa at Newport, Isle of Wight', Antiq J 9 (1929)

Swain, E.J. 1979   K.A.A. Excavations, The Chessals, Kingscote, 1979

Swan, V.G. 1984   The Pottery kilns of Roman Britain, H.M.S.O. London, 1984

Tatton-Brown, T. 1980   Note in Britannia II (1980)

Tomalin, D.J. 1975   Newport Roman Villa, Newport, 1975

Tomlin, R. 1979   'Graffiti on Roman bricks and tiles found in Britain', Brit Archaeol Rep 68 (1979)

Toynbee, J.M.C. 1964   Art in Britain under the Romans, Oxford, 1964

Tucker, C. 1848 — 'Notice of Roman remains lately discovered in Lower Thames St.', Archaeol J 5 (1848)

van Buren, E.D. 1941 — Note in 'American Journal of Archaeology' 45 (1941)

Victoria County History — Essex, vol. iii, London, 1963

Victoria County History — Hertfordshire, vol. iv, London, 1914

Walters, H.B. 1905 — A History of Ancient Pottery, vol. ii, London, 1905

Ward, J. 1909 — 'The Roman Fort of Gellygaer – The Baths', Trans Cardiff Natur Soc 42 (1909)

Ward, J. 1911 — 'Romano-British Buildings and Earthworks', London, 1911

Ward-Perkins, J.B. & Toynbee, J.M.C. 1949 — 'The Hunting Baths at Lepcis Magna', Archaeologia 93 (1949)

Ward-Perkins, J.B. 1981 — Roman Imperial Architecture, London, 1981

Webster, G. 1960 — 'The Roman town bath-house', The Chester Historian, 10 (1960)

Webster, G. 1963 — Practical Archaeology, London, 1963

Webster, J. 1775 — 'The construction of the old wall at Verulam', Archaeologia 2 (1775)

Wellbeloved, C. 1842 — Eburacum, York, 1842

West, S. & Plouviez, J. 1976 — 'The Romano-British site at Icklingham', E Anglian Archaeol Report no. 3, 1976

Wheeler, R.E.M. 1926 — 'The Roman Fort near Brecon', Y Cymmrodor 37 (1926)

Wheeler, R.E.M. 1932 — 'Notes on building construction in Roman Britain', J Roman Stud 22 (1932)

Wheeler, R.E.M. & Wheeler, T.V. 1936 — Verulamium : a Belgic and two Roman cities (Soc Ant Report XI), Oxford, 1936

Williams, F.H. 1895 — 'Deva – traces of a building discovered west of the Forum', J Brit Archaeol Ass I (n Ser) (1895)

Williams, J.H. 1971 — 'Roman building materials in the southwest', Trans Bristol Gloucestershire Archaeol Soc 90 (1971)

Wilson, R.J.A. 1979 — 'Brick and Tiles in Roman Sicily', Brit Archaeol Rep 68 (1979)

Wilson, M.G. 1984 — 'Relief Pattern Flue Tiles', Verulamium Excavations iii, O.U.C.A. Monograph I, 1984

Winbolt, S.E. 1922 — 'Alfoldean Roman Station', Sussex Archaeol Collect 64 (1922)

Winbolt, S.E. & Goodchild, R.G. 1937 — 'A Roman villa at Lickfold, Wiggonholt', Sussex Archaeol Collect 76 (1937)

Winbolt, S.E. & Goodchild, R.G. 1940 — 'The Roman villa at Lickfold, Wiggonholt', Sussex Archaeol Collect 81 (1940)

Wright, F.S. 1939   'Report of bricks and tiles found at Highdown', Sussex Archaeol Collect 80 (1939)

Young, C. 1979   'The Processing of Roman Tiles', Brit Archaeol Rep 68 (1979)

Bibliography of material concerning stamped tile

THE LEGIONS

Legio II Augusta	V.E. Nash-Williams	'The Legionary Fortress at Caerleon in Monmouthshire', Archaeol Cambrensis 87, 1932, 53–8
Legio II	G.C. Boon	Laterarium Iscanum, the Antefixes, Brick and Tile Stamps of the Second Augustan Legion, National Museum of Wales, 1984
Legio VI	R.P. Wright	'Tile stamps of the Sixth Legion found in Britain', Britannia 7, 1976, 224–235
Legio IX	R.P. Wright	'Tile stamps of the Ninth Legion found in Britain', Britannia 9, 1978, 379–382
Legio XX	W.F. Grimes	'Holt, Denbighshire, The works depot of the 20th Legion at Castle Lyons', Y Cymmrodor, vol. 41, 1930
Legio VIII	D. Baatz	'Stamps of the 8th Legion at Saalburg', Saalburg-Jahrbuch, 27 (1970)
	M.W.C. Hassall	'Military tile stamps from Britain' Brit Archaeol Rep 68, 1979, 261–6
	A.D. McWhirr	'Origins of Legionary tile stamping in Britain' Brit Archaeol Rep 68, 1979, 253–59

THE CLASSIS BRITANNICA

G. Brodribb   'Stamped tiles of the Classis Britannica' Sussex Archaeol Collect 107, 1969, 102–25

D.P.S. Peacock	'Bricks and Tiles of the Classis Britannica; Petrology & Origin', Britannia 8, 1977
G. Brodribb	'A further study of stamped tiles of the Classis Britannica', Sussex Archaeol Collect, 118, 1980, 183–196
W. Williams	in B. Philp's 'Excavations of the Roman Forts of the Classis Britannica at Dover', 1981, 123–42

STAMPS FROM THE COTSWOLD AREA

E.H. Clifford	'Stamped tiles found in Gloucestershire', J Roman Stud 45, 1955, 68–72
A. McWhirr & D. Viner	'The production and distribution of tiles in Roman Britain with particular reference to the Cirencester region', Britannia 9, 1978, 359–77
T. Darvill	'A petrological study of LHS and TPF stamped tiles from the Cotswold region', Brit Archaeol Rep 68, 1979, 309–351
T. Darvill	'Some small groups of stamped Roman ceramic tiles from the Cotswolds', Glevensis 14, 1980, 49–57
C.M. Heighway & A.J. Parker	'The Roman tilery at St Oswald's Priory, Gloucester', Britannia 13, 1982, 25–77
T. Darvill & A.D. McWhirr	'Brick and tile production in Roman Britain : models of economic organisation', World Archaeology, Vol 15–3, 1984, 239–261

also :

M. Todd	Roman stamped tiles from Lincoln and their origin, Lincolnshire Hist Archaeol, I, 1966, 29–31
R.P. Wright	'Official Tile stamps from London which cite the Province of Britain', Britannia 16, 1985, 193–6
T.P. Wiseman	'Tile stamps and Roman nomenclature', Brit Archaeol Rep 68, 1979, 221–6